SENIDLILE KODWA?

Have you eaten yet?

ZANELE VAN ZYL

SENIDLILE KODWA?

Have you eaten yet?

ACKNOWLEDGEMENTS

To my husband, who has been a consistent support on this amazing journey.

To my children, Thando and Zandi, for encouraging me to always reach for more, and for seeing potential in me even when I wanted to settle.

To my right hand, my manager, Mabatho Mutloatse, for being the energy that makes it all happen.

To the team at Penguin Random House SA for helping to make this book a reality, thank you to Bev, Aimee, Randall, Cecilia, Henk and Emma.

To my social-media family, for believing in my brand and embracing me with such excitement. I'm humbled.

To the brands I'm privileged to collaborate with, thank you for your faith in me and the opportunity to grow together.

CONTENTS

SENIDLILE KODWA? Have you eaten yet?........ 9

BREAKFAST & BRUNCH 11

VEGETARIAN & SALADS 29

MEAT, CHICKEN & SEAFOOD 47

SUNDAY SPREAD 93

HOME GROWN 111

ELEVATE YOUR MEAL:
Sauces, Dressings, Dips & Marinades.... 123

SOMETHING ON THE SIDE 141

NIBBLES 153

BAKERY 169

SWEET TREATS & DRINKS 189

RECIPE INDEX 202

SENIDLILE KODWA?
Have you eaten yet?

Welcome to my third cookbook – we did it again, folks!

The question, 'Senidlile kodwa?', is an expression of my love language, the joy I find in preparing food for other people. I am much like my mother, aunties, grandmothers, and all the women in my family – nobody is allowed to leave my house hungry. If they don't eat, I will surely send them off with a skaftin.

I've learnt that it is our uniqueness as individuals that makes life interesting, and people appreciate authenticity. Staying true to who I am – a village girl – works for me, whether in the culinary world or just life in general. Knowing who you are and where you come from will help to pave your pathway through life. And so the title of this book, *Senidlile Kodwa?*, is a reflection of my identity, what I stand for, and how this has carried me through my journey with food.

Based on this saying, 'Senidlile kodwa?', one that is steeped in my heritage and upbringing, this book is a celebration of food and the people who helped me get to where I am today. Food is a universal language, so even if you don't speak or understand isiZulu, I am confident that everyone around the world will be able to understand the emotion behind the phrase. I hope you see this book as a love letter from me to you and your loved ones.

By the way, senidlile kodwa? Hahaha! I hope not, because we are about to enjoy all these scrumptious recipes made with love...

BREAKFAST & BRUNCH

I've heard that breakfast is the most important meal of the day. I totally agree, which is why I always make my breakfast cheery and colourful to brighten up my morning. This chapter is filled with tasty and easy-to-follow recipes to kickstart your day.

GRANOLA

SERVES 10–12

4 cups rolled oats
1 cup sesame seeds
1 cup pumpkin seeds
2 cups raw unsalted mixed nuts
1 cup honey
1 cup dried cranberries

Preheat the oven to 180°C.

In a bowl, combine the oats, sesame seeds, pumpkin seeds, mixed nuts and honey. Spread the mixture evenly on a greased baking tray.

Bake for 25 minutes, then mix in the cranberries. Bake for another 10 minutes, or until lightly golden. Remove the granola from the oven and allow to cool completely. Serve for breakfast or any time as a snack. Store in an airtight container for 1–2 weeks, or in the freezer for up to 3 months.

CHICKEN AND BACON CRUSTLESS MINI QUICHES

MAKES 6–9

2 Tbsp oil
4 eggs
1 cup fresh cream
1 cup cooked and shredded chicken
1 cup chopped cooked bacon
1 cup mixed diced (and pith removed) green, yellow and red peppers

Preheat the oven to 180°C. Grease a 12-cup muffin tray with oil.

In a bowl, whisk together the eggs and fresh cream. Mix in the shredded chicken, bacon and peppers.

Pour the mixture into the muffin tray cups. Bake for 12–15 minutes, or until the egg has set. Remove the quiches from the tray. Allow to cool for 5 minutes before serving.

PEANUT BUTTER OATS

I enjoy oats at any time of the day. They are so filling and I like exploring ways to make them tastier, like adding peanut butter and cinnamon.

SERVES 2

2 cups water
1 tsp salt
1 cup rolled oats
4 Tbsp peanut butter, divided
2 Tbsp honey, divided
2 tsp ground cinnamon

In a small saucepan over medium heat, bring the water to a boil and add the salt. Stir in the oats and cook for 5 minutes, stirring frequently to prevent them from sticking to the bottom of the saucepan and burning. Remove from the heat.

Divide the cooked oats evenly between 2 bowls, then add 2 tablespoons of peanut butter and 1 tablespoon of honey to each. Sprinkle 1 teaspoon of cinnamon over each bowl. Serve warm.

TOMATO SHAKSHUKA

SERVES 4

2 Tbsp oil
1 medium onion, chopped
2 Tbsp tomato paste
1 Tbsp origanum
1 Tbsp barbecue spice
2 × 410g cans chopped tomatoes
Salt and pepper, to taste
4 eggs

Heat the oil in a pan over medium heat. Add the onion and sauté until golden brown, then mix in the tomato paste. Add the origanum and barbecue spice, then stir in the chopped tomatoes. Season with salt and pepper, then simmer for 6–8 minutes, or until the liquid has reduced.

Use a spoon to make 4 small wells in the tomato sauce and crack an egg into each one. Cover the pan with a lid and continue to simmer over low heat for 5–8 minutes, or until the eggs are done to your liking. Garnish as desired and enjoy with a crisp bread of your choice.

CHICKEN QUESADILLA

SERVES 2-4

2 Tbsp oil
2 chicken breast fillets, diced
1 Tbsp chilli powder
1 Tbsp garlic powder
1 small onion, diced
1 red pepper, diced and pith removed
4 tortillas
3 cups grated mozzarella cheese, divided

Heat the oil in a large pan over medium heat. Add the chicken, and sprinkle with the chilli powder and garlic powder. Stir in the onion and red pepper, then cook until the vegetables are soft and the chicken is browned and cooked through. Set aside.

Heat a nonstick pan over medium heat. Place 1 tortilla in the pan and toast for 2 minutes on each side. Add some of the chicken filling to the centre of the tortilla and top with some grated mozzarella cheese. Fold over the tortilla and continue to cook until the cheese has melted. Remove from the pan and repeat with the remaining tortillas and chicken mixture. Slice the quesadillas before serving, or enjoy them as is.

VEGETARIAN OMELETTE

SERVES 1

3 eggs
10g butter
1 cup sliced mushrooms
1 cup baby spinach
1 cup mixed diced (and pith removed) green, yellow and red peppers
1 Tbsp vegetable seasoning
½ cup grated cheese of your choice

Crack the eggs into a bowl and beat using a whisk or electric mixer. Set aside.

In a nonstick pan, melt the butter over medium heat. Add the mushrooms, spinach and peppers, then sauté until softened. Stir through the vegetable seasoning, then remove the mixture from the pan. With the pan still on the heat, pour in the beaten eggs and allow to sit for a minute, until the edges are set. Add the vegetable mixture to one side of the omelette and top with the grated cheese. When the egg begins to set, use a spatula to gently lift the cooked egg from the edges of the pan. Fold one half of the omelette over the other to enclose the filling. Cook for a few more seconds, or until the cheese has melted.

PICKLED FISH

SERVES 8–10

¼ cup cake wheat flour
Salt and pepper, to taste
1kg hake fillets
4 cups oil, plus 2 Tbsp
2 large onions, sliced into rings
1 clove garlic, minced
1 tsp minced or grated fresh ginger
1 Tbsp black peppercorns
1 Tbsp ground cardamom
3–4 red chillies, seeds removed (optional), and chopped
3–4 bay leaves
1 tsp medium curry powder
1 tsp ground turmeric
1 tsp ground cumin
1 tsp white pepper
2 Tbsp sugar
½ cup white spirit vinegar
½ cup lemon juice
Zest of 1 lemon
3 sprigs fresh thyme

In a large bowl, combine the flour, and salt and pepper. Dip the hake fillets in the seasoned flour to coat on both sides.

Heat 4 cups of oil over medium heat in a deep pan and fry the fish for 2–5 minutes on each side, depending on the thickness of the fillet (do not overcook), until golden brown. Remove from the pan and transfer to a plate lined with paper towel.

In a separate pan, heat the remaining 2 tablespoons of oil over medium heat. Fry the onion rings, garlic and ginger. Add the peppercorns, cardamom, chopped chillies, bay leaves, curry powder, turmeric, cumin and white pepper. Stir in the sugar, vinegar, lemon juice, lemon zest, more salt and pepper, and thyme. Cook until the sugar has dissolved.

Place the fried fish in the pan and stir gently until coated all over. Transfer to a dish, cover with cling wrap and refrigerate overnight. Serve with Soft Bread Rolls (see p. 146).

MY CHILDREN AND I ARE IN THE KITCHEN

I have two beautiful children: Thando, my eldest, and Zandi, my youngest. They have very different tastes when it comes to food. Of course, between the two of them, there can be lots of arguments in the kitchen, whether it is Thando complaining about the amount of onion in a dish or Zandi trying to teach her big sister how to crush garlic. I don't always involve myself in their arguments, because I know I have the last say, anyway. All I have to do is ask, 'Who is the chef in this kitchen?', and that's the end of that!

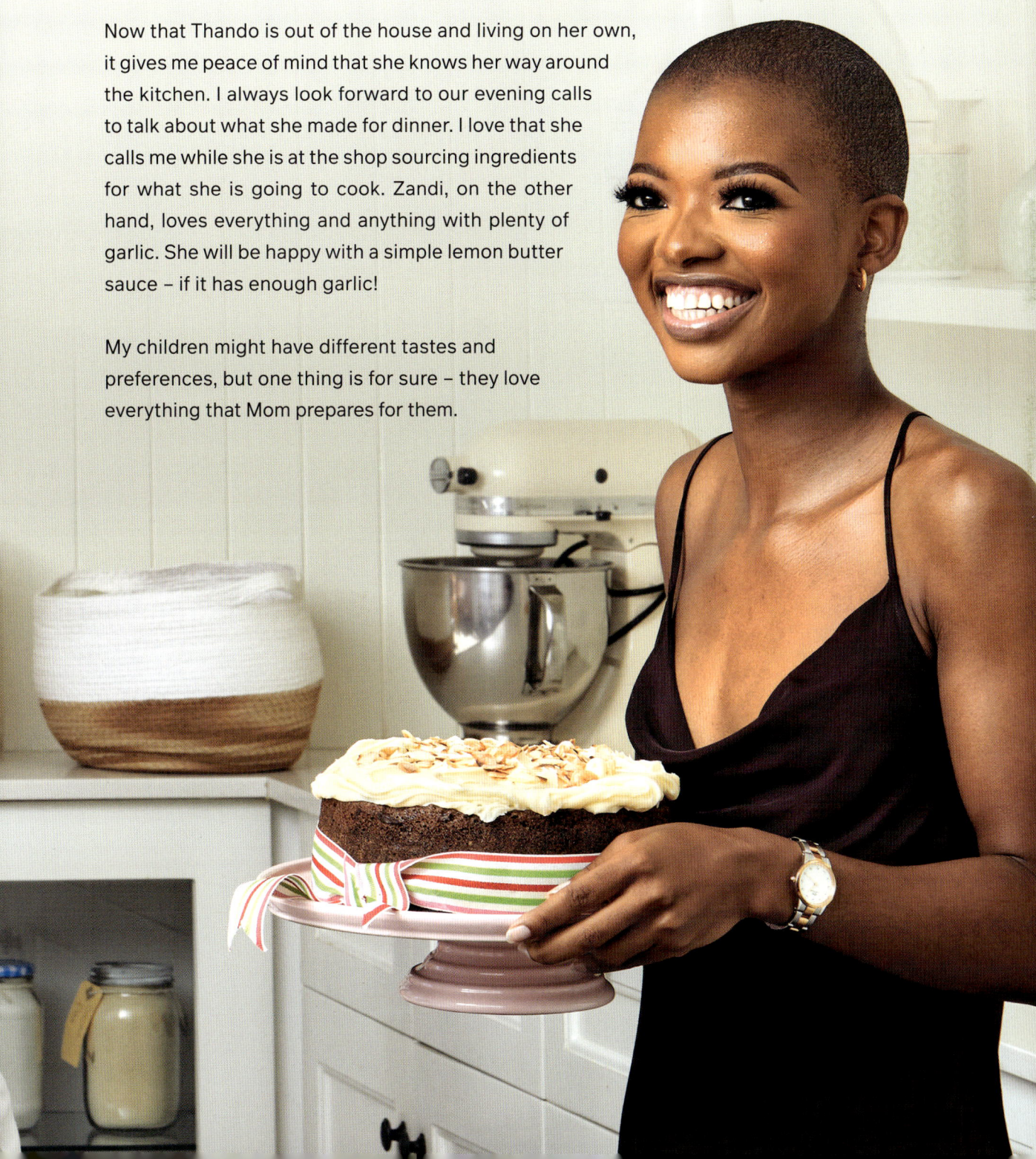

I strongly believe we should teach children the basics of cooking while they are still young. This way, when they grow up, they will feel comfortable in the kitchen, and they won't find cooking frustrating or daunting. After all, cooking should be fun and enjoyable.

Now that Thando is out of the house and living on her own, it gives me peace of mind that she knows her way around the kitchen. I always look forward to our evening calls to talk about what she made for dinner. I love that she calls me while she is at the shop sourcing ingredients for what she is going to cook. Zandi, on the other hand, loves everything and anything with plenty of garlic. She will be happy with a simple lemon butter sauce – if it has enough garlic!

My children might have different tastes and preferences, but one thing is for sure – they love everything that Mom prepares for them.

VEGETARIAN & SALADS

If I'm honest, I was that child who had to be bribed to eat her vegetables. But I think it's because people would usually overcook them. Now that I've learnt how to perfect my vegetarian dishes, they are my favourite.

BLANCHED VEGGIES

SERVES 4

300g vegetably medley (I used baby marrows, cauliflower and broccoli, but butternut, sweet potato and carrots will also work)

Bring a pot of water (about 4 cups) to a boil. Add the vegetables and boil for 2–3 minutes. Remove from the heat, drain and place the vegetables in a bowl of ice water, until they cool down. Drain the vegetables and serve as a side.

> **NOTE** Blanching is a cooking technique in which vegetables are cooked briefly over heat, then plunged immediately into ice water to halt the cooking process. This helps vegetables to retain their colour, preserve their nutrients and keep them crisp.

VEGETABLE LASAGNE

SERVES 4–6

2 Tbsp olive oil
1 onion, finely chopped
3 cloves garlic, minced
Handful fresh thyme
2 Tbsp tomato paste
1 each red, green and yellow peppers, roughly chopped
2 medium zucchini, diced
2 medium potatoes, peeled and diced
1 butternut, peeled and cubed
1 × 410g can chopped tomatoes
2 cups vegetable stock
1 × 250g packet lasagne sheets
1 cup grated cheddar cheese or mozzarella cheese

FOR THE BÉCHAMEL SAUCE

30g butter
2 Tbsp flour
400ml milk
Salt and pepper, to taste

Heat the oil in a pot over medium heat. Add the onion, garlic and thyme, then sauté until the onion is golden and caramelised. Stir in the tomato paste, then add the peppers, zucchini, potatoes, butternut, canned tomatoes and stock. Simmer over low heat for 12–15 minutes, or until the vegetables are soft and the liquid has reduced.

To make the béchamel sauce, melt the butter in a small saucepan over low heat. Whisk in the flour, then slowly add the milk, stirring frequently. Season with salt and pepper. Bring it to a gentle simmer and cook until the sauce is smooth and thick, stirring frequently to avoid lumps.

In the meantime, preheat the oven to 180°C and boil the lasagne sheets for 3–5 minutes.

To assemble the lasagne, layer the cooked lasagne sheets at the bottom of a casserole dish. Spoon over a layer of the cooked vegetables, followed by a layer of the white sauce. Keep layering in this way until you've used all the ingredients, finishing with a final layer of white sauce. Top with the grated cheese, then bake for 12–15 minutes, or until the cheese is melted and golden brown.

BROWN RICE AND HALLOUMI SALAD

SERVES 4

1 Tbsp olive oil
200g halloumi cheese, cut into strips or cubes
2 cups cooked brown rice
1 red onion, chopped
1 cup chopped cucumber
1 Tbsp grated fresh ginger
Handful fresh coriander, finely chopped

FOR THE DRESSING

3 Tbsp lemon juice
3 Tbsp olive oil
1 clove garlic, minced
Salt and pepper, to taste

Heat a pan over medium heat and add the olive oil. Add the halloumi and fry on all sides until golden brown. Remove from the heat.

In a salad bowl, gently mix the rice, onion, cucumber, ginger, coriander and fried halloumi. Alternatively, place the halloumi on top of the other ingredients.

To make the dressing, mix all the dressing ingredients until well combined. Pour over the salad and toss to coat.

STEAMED GREEN VEGGIES
WITH HONEY-MUSTARD DRESSING

SERVES 6

1–1.5kg mixed vegetables (such as asparagus, long-stem broccoli, baby carrots, sugar snap peas)

FOR THE HONEY-MUSTARD DRESSING
5 Tbsp lemon juice
2 cloves garlic, minced
2 tsp wholegrain mustard
2 tsp honey
½ cup melted butter
Salt and pepper, to taste

Steam the vegetables in a colander over a pot of simmering water for 5 minutes, or until tender-crisp. Arrange the vegetables on a platter.

To make the dressing, mix together the lemon juice, garlic, mustard, honey, melted butter, and salt and pepper until combined. Pour the dressing over the steamed vegetables and serve immediately.

TOMATO AND HERB SALAD

SERVES 4

2 cups cherry tomatoes, cut into halves
½ cup finely chopped red onion
¼ cup finely chopped fresh basil leaves, plus extra sprigs to garnish
¼ cup finely chopped fresh parsley
¼ cup finely chopped chives
2 Tbsp olive oil
2 Tbsp thick balsamic vinegar
Handful crumbled feta cheese

On a serving platter, arrange the tomatoes, onion, chopped basil, parsley and chives.

Drizzle over the olive oil and balsamic vinegar, then sprinkle over the crumbled feta cheese. Garnish with basil sprigs.

BEAN AND CHICKPEA BULGUR WHEAT SALAD

SERVES 2

1 cup bulgur wheat
1 cup boiling hot vegetable stock
1 cup chopped cucumber
1 medium red onion, diced
1 × 410g can red kidney beans, drained
1 × 410g can chickpeas, drained
1 red pepper, pith removed, and diced
Handful each fresh coriander and dill, finely chopped

FOR THE DRESSING

2 Tbsp olive oil
2 Tbsp balsamic vinegar

Add the bulgur wheat to a bowl and pour over the vegetable stock. Cover with cling wrap and leave for 15–20 minutes, to allow the bulgur wheat to cook gently in the heat of the stock. Fluff the cooked bulgur wheat with a fork.

To the cooked bulgur wheat, add the cucumber, onion, kidney beans, chickpeas, red pepper and fresh herbs. Gently mix using a fork.

To make the dressing, mix together the olive oil and balsamic vinegar. Pour the dressing over the salad just before serving.

THE GREEN SALAD

I love the colour and textures of this salad. When I make salads, I usually use what I have in my fridge and pantry. I tried this one recently and my family loved it. All the shades of green, flavours and textures combine perfectly.

SERVES 6

3 kiwi fruit, peeled and sliced
200g fresh rocket
1 cup green olives, pits removed
1 avocado, diced

FOR THE DRESSING

2 Tbsp white balsamic vinegar
1 Tbsp olive oil
1 clove garlic, minced
1 red chilli, seeds removed, and finely chopped (optional)
Handful fresh coriander, finely chopped

In a salad bowl, gently mix the kiwi fruit, rocket, olives and avocado.

To make the dressing, combine all the dressing ingredients. Drizzle it over the salad just before serving.

MUSHROOM RISOTTO

SERVES 3

2 Tbsp oil
60g butter
1 small onion, chopped
3 cloves garlic, minced
1 Tbsp chopped fresh thyme
250g white button mushrooms, sliced
1 cup arborio (risotto) rice
2 cups vegetable stock
1 cup white wine
1 cup grated parmesan cheese
1 cup fresh cream
Handful chopped chives, to garnish

In a pan over medium heat, heat the oil and butter. Add the onion, garlic and thyme, and fry for 2–3 minutes, or until fragrant. Add the mushrooms and cook until browned.

Stir through the arborio rice, then pour in the vegetable stock and wine. Cook, covered with a lid, over low heat for 15–20 minutes, stirring frequently, until the rice is tender. Remove from the heat. Stir in the parmesan cheese and fresh cream, then garnish with chives and serve.

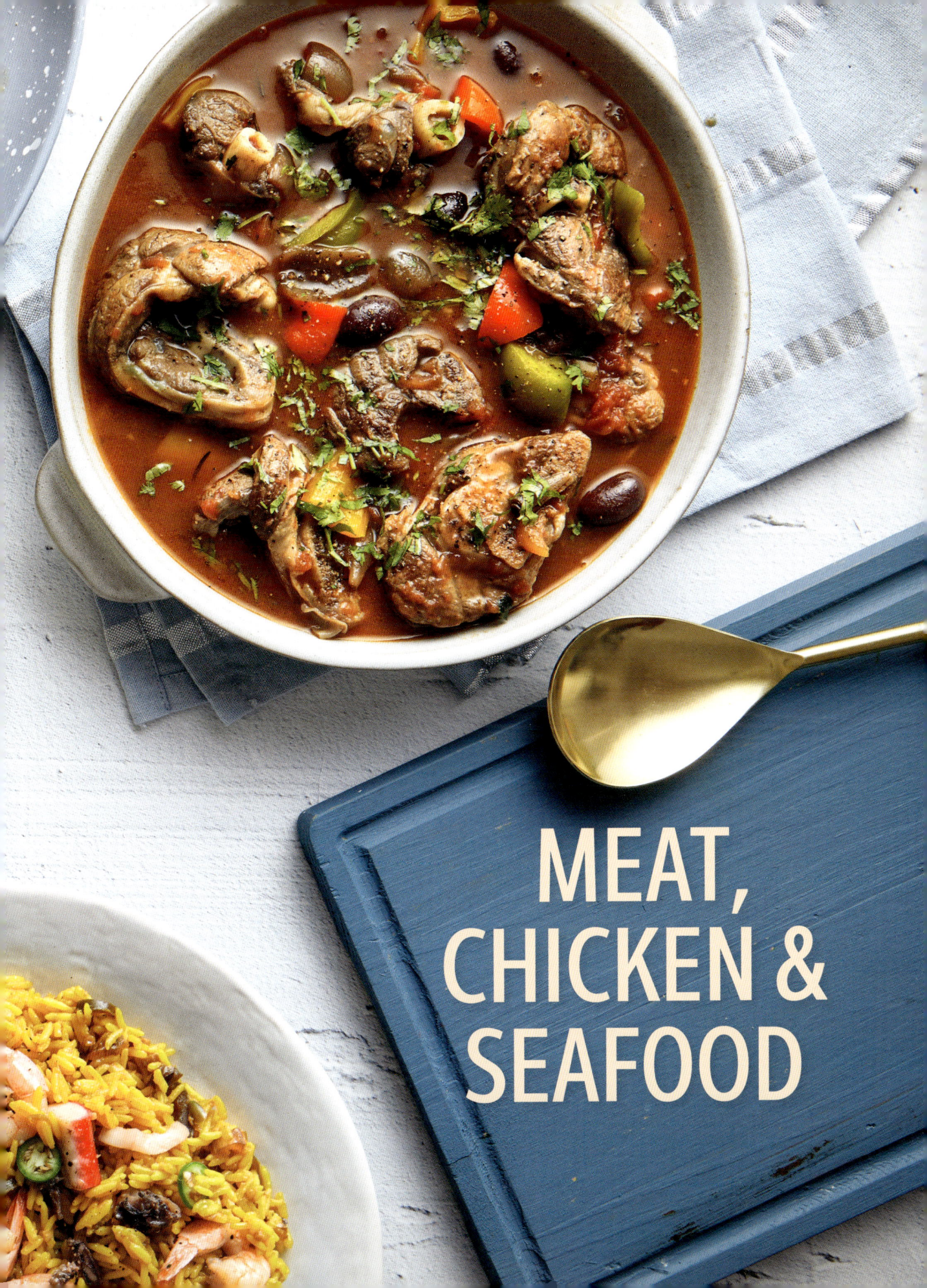

MEAT, CHICKEN & SEAFOOD

MEAT

LAMB KNUCKLE STEW

This hearty, tasty, wholesome and colourful stew will take you back to your mom's kitchen, and keep your family warm. I love the natural flavour of lamb and this easy-to-prepare recipe is one of my favourites.

SERVES 6–8

20ml oil
Handful chopped fresh rosemary
1kg lamb knuckles
1 Tbsp barbecue spice
1 tsp paprika
1 cup drained cocktail pickled onions
1 cup pitted olives
1 mutton stock cube dissolved in 2 cups boiling water
1 × 410g can chopped tomatoes
1 each red, green and yellow pepper, pith removed, and cut into chunks
Salt and pepper, to taste

Heat the oil in a pan over medium heat. Fry the rosemary until fragrant, then remove from the oil and set aside.

To the same pan, add the lamb knuckles and fry until browned. Season with the barbecue spice and paprika. Mix in the pickled onions and olives, then pour in the stock and stir through the tomatoes. Simmer for 1 hour over low heat, stirring occasionally to avoid sticking. Add more stock or water, if necessary. Add the peppers and fried rosemary, and cook for 10–15 minutes, or until the lamb is soft. Garnish with any chopped herbs of your choosing and serve hot with Uphuthu (see p. 121), rice, mashed potatoes, dumplings or samp.

LAMB KEBABS
IN A HERBY YOGHURT SAUCE

SERVES 4

4 wooden skewers
500g leg of lamb, cut into cubes
1 Tbsp garlic powder
4 Tbsp olive oil, divided
2 cloves garlic, minced
¼ cup balsamic vinegar
½ cup plain yoghurt
Handful fresh mint, finely chopped, plus extra leaves, to garnish
Handful fresh parsley, chopped

In a large enough dish or bowl, cover the wooden skewers with boiling water. Leave for a few minutes, then remove and set aside (see Tip).

Season the lamb with garlic powder. Thread the cubes of lamb onto the skewers, about 4–6 cubes per skewer. Heat 2 tablespoons of olive oil in a pan over medium heat, and sear the lamb kebabs (they will be cooked further in the sauce later). Remove from the pan and set aside.

Turn the heat down to low and heat the remaining olive oil in the same pan. Add the garlic and sauté for 1 minute, or until fragrant. Stir in the balsamic vinegar, yoghurt, mint and parsley, and simmer for 4 minutes. Return the kebabs to the pan and let them simmer in the sauce for a further 4 minutes. Garnish with mint leaves and serve with mashed potatoes or fried rice.

> **TIP** This will prevent the wooden skewers from burning when you cook the lamb.

LAMB AND BUTTERNUT PASTA

SERVES 4

250g butternut, peeled, and cubed
2 Tbsp oil, divided
1 Tbsp vegetable seasoning
400g leg of lamb, cut into small cubes or strips
1 medium onion, chopped
2 cloves garlic, minced
100g sun-dried tomatoes
Salt and pepper, to taste
300g cooked penne pasta
2 Tbsp chopped fresh chives or parsley, to garnish

FOR THE BÉCHAMEL SAUCE

30g butter
2 Tbsp flour
400ml fresh milk
Salt and pepper, to taste

Preheat the oven to 180°C.

Arrange the butternut on a oven tray, drizzle with 1 tablespoon of oil and season with the vegetable seasoning. Roast in the oven for 10–12 minutes, until cooked through and golden. Remove from the oven and set aside.

In a pan over medium heat, heat the remaining oil, then brown the lamb pieces. Once the lamb is browned, add the onion, garlic and sun-dried tomatoes. Season with salt and pepper, then stir through the cooked pasta and butternut. Set aside.

To make the béchamel sauce, melt the butter in a saucepan over low heat. Add the flour and whisk well until there are no lumps. Slowly pour in the milk, whisking continuously, and allow the mixture to simmer, adding extra milk, if the mixture is too thick and lumpy. Season with salt and pepper, then set aside.

Pour the béchamel sauce over the pasta and stir gently until well coated. Season with more salt and pepper, if you like, and garnish with fresh chives or parsley.

THYME AND MUSTARD LAMB CHOPS

SERVES 6

2 Tbsp lemon juice
2 Tbsp chopped fresh thyme, plus extra sprigs to garnish
2 cloves garlic, chopped
1 Tbsp olive oil
Salt and pepper, to taste
6 lamb chops
3 tsp Dijon or English mustard
1 cup white wine

In a bowl, mix together the lemon juice, thyme, garlic, olive oil, and salt and pepper. Place the lamb chops in this marinade, and leave to marinate for 1 hour or overnight.

Heat a pan over medium heat. Remove the lamb chops from the marinade (reserve the marinade) using a fork or braai tongs. Place them in the pan and sear for 1 minute on both sides. Pour the reserved marinade over the lamb chops. Use a fork or whisk to mix together the mustard and wine in the same bowl. Pour it over the chops and cook for 3–5 minutes, or until the mixture reduces and thickens. Season with extra salt and pepper, if you like and garnish with sprigs of thyme.

MUTTON BUNNY CHOW

SERVES 4

Dash of oil
1kg boneless mutton, cut into cubes
1 onion, finely chopped
4 cloves garlic, finely chopped
2 tsp fresh ginger, finely chopped
Pinch masala spice or hot curry powder
2 tsp chilli powder
2 tsp ground coriander
2 Tbsp ground cumin
1 tsp cayenne pepper (optional)
2 × 410g cans chopped tomatoes
4 medium potatoes, peeled, and diced
1 tsp salt
½ tsp ground black pepper
1 loaf fresh white bread, uncut
1 punnet fresh coriander leaves, roughly chopped to garnish

Heat the oil in a deep pot over high heat. Add the mutton cubes and fry until browned, then remove from the pot.

Lower the heat to medium. To the same pot, add the onion, garlic and ginger, and fry for 5 minutes, or until the onion is soft. Stir in the masala spice or curry powder, chilli powder, ground coriander, ground cumin and cayenne pepper, and fry for 1–2 minutes. Return the mutton to the pot and cook for about 3 minutes.

Stir in the chopped tomatoes, potatoes, and salt and black pepper. Keep stirring, scraping the bottom of the pot with a spoon to loosen any sticky bits. Cover with a lid and simmer over medium-low heat for about 30 minutes, stirring now and again so that the bottom of the pot doesn't burn. Then, cook uncovered for a few minutes to allow the sauce to reduce and thicken. Remove the pot from the heat and add some more salt and pepper to taste, if you like.

Cut the loaf of bread into quarters. Scoop or cut out the centres of each quarter loaf (but not all the way through), essentially creating a 'bowl' of bread for the curry. Fill the hole of each quarter loaf with the mutton curry. Garnish with fresh coriander and serve.

BEEF CURRY

SERVES 6

1kg beef cubes or beef goulash
1 cup mayonnaise
20ml oil
2 cloves garlic, minced
1 onion, chopped
1 Tbsp grated fresh ginger
1 Tbsp medium curry powder
1 Tbsp ground cumin
1 tsp paprika
1 tsp ground turmeric
1 Tbsp ground coriander
2 cups beef stock
½ cup plain yoghurt
Salt and pepper, to taste
Handful fresh coriander

Add the beef cubes and mayonnaise to a dish, stir to coat, then set aside to marinate for 30–60 minutes or, ideally, overnight.

Heat the oil in a pot over medium heat, then add the garlic, onion and ginger, and sauté until fragrant. Add the marinated beef cubes, curry powder, ground cumin, paprika, turmeric and coriander, and stir. Fry for 2–3 minutes, being careful not to burn the spices. Pour in the stock, lower the heat, and simmer for 40–45 minutes, until the liquid reduces and the beef is tender. Stir in the yoghurt, and season with salt and pepper. Simmer for a further 5–8 minutes. Garnish with fresh coriander, and serve with rice or roti.

RUMP STEAK
WITH MUSHROOM SAUCE

SERVES 1

FOR THE MUSHROOM SAUCE

1 Tbsp flour
100ml milk
30g butter
1 onion, chopped
2 cloves garlic, minced
250g white button mushrooms, sliced
2 sprigs fresh thyme
1 cup fresh cream
Salt and pepper, to taste

FOR THE STEAK

1 tsp ground black pepper
1 tsp dried chilli flakes
1 tsp dried origanum
1 tsp garlic powder
1 tsp brown sugar
1 tsp paprika
1 tsp salt
30g butter
2 cloves garlic
4 sprigs fresh thyme
1 × 300g rump steak

For the mushroom sauce, mix the flour and milk in a small bowl or jug, then set aside.

Melt the butter in a pan over medium heat. Add the onion and garlic, and sauté for 2–3 minutes, or until fragrant. Add the mushrooms and thyme, and stir until the mushrooms are golden brown. Pour in the fresh cream and lower the heat. Stir in the flour and milk mixture. Season with salt and pepper, and cook for 3 minutes, or until the sauce has thickened. Remove from the heat and set aside.

To prepare the steak, make a dry rub by mixing together the ground black pepper, chilli flakes, origanum, garlic powder, brown sugar, paprika and salt. Rub the mixture all over the steak.

Add the butter to a pan and melt over high heat. Add the garlic cloves and sprigs of thyme, and fry for 1 minute. Place the steak in the pan and fry for 3 minutes on each side, or to your liking (see Tip). Remove from the pan and allow the steak to rest for 5–7 minutes, to allow the juices to distribute.

In the meantime, reheat the mushroom sauce over low–medium heat. Then, pour the sauce over the steak and serve.

TIP

I prefer my steak medium, but follow the cooking times below to cook the steak to your preference.

RARE = 2 minutes per side

MEDIUM = 3 minutes per side

WELL DONE = 6 minutes per side

SPICY OX LIVER

SERVES 4

1 Tbsp oil
1 medium onion, sliced
2 cloves garlic, minced
1 tsp paprika
1 Tbsp hot curry powder
1 chilli, seeds removed, and finely chopped
4 small pieces (200–250g per piece) ox liver
½ cup plain yoghurt
Salt and pepper, to taste

In a pan, heat the oil over medium heat. Add the onion and garlic, and sauté for 2 minutes. Add the paprika and curry powder. Cook until fragrant, then add the chopped chillies. Lower the heat. Add the ox liver and cook for 2 minutes on each side (avoid cooking the liver for longer, to prevent it from becoming tough – remember the blood adds flavour). Add the yogurt, salt and pepper. Cook for another 2 minutes, then serve with mashed potatoes or Uphuthu (see p. 121).

PULLED PORK BELLY BURGER

SERVES 4

1 kg boneless pork belly
1 medium onion, finely chopped
½ cup apricot jam
⅓ cup Worcestershire sauce
4 cloves garlic, finely chopped
2 Tbsp grated ginger
2 red chillies, seeds removed, and finely chopped
½ cup white grape vinegar
½ cup apple cider vinegar
1 Tbsp chicken spice
1 tsp paprika

TO SERVE

4 hamburger buns
2 cups shredded rainbow cabbage

Preheat the oven to 180°C.

Place the pork belly in a big enough pot, add the onion and cover with water. Boil for 30–45 minutes, or until cooked through. Remove the pork belly from the water and set aside.

In a small saucepan, combine the apricot jam, Worcestershire sauce, garlic, ginger, chillies, white vinegar, apple cider vinegar, chicken spice and paprika. Cook over low heat until the sauce has reduced to a thick glaze.

Place the pork belly in a roasting dish. Remove the skin. Pour the glaze over the pork belly, making sure it is coated all over. Bake in the oven for 15 minutes, or until tender enough to easily shred or pull apart.

Use two forks to shred the pork belly. Divide the shredded pork and cabbage evenly among the 4 hamburger buns, and serve.

SWEET AND SOUR PORK CHOPS

My go-to, quick-fix recipe after a long day, this dish always saves the day, and can be served with mashed potatoes or pasta salad.

SERVES 4

4 pork chops
2 Tbsp chicken spice
1 Tbsp olive oil
100ml lemon juice
3 Tbsp honey
1 Tbsp dried chilli flakes
2 cloves garlic, minced

Season the pork chops on both sides with the chicken spice. Heat the olive oil in a pan over medium heat and add the pork chops. Fry until browned on both sides, then remove and set aside.

To the same pan, add the lemon juice, honey, chilli flakes and garlic. Simmer for 2–3 minutes, or until the sauce has reduced, then return the pork chops to the pan. Cook for 4–6 minutes. Garnish as desired, then serve.

STUFFED PORK FILLET

SERVES 5–6

2 kg pork fillet
1 Tbsp finely chopped fresh red chilli (seeds removed)
1 onion, finely chopped
200g baby spinach, chopped
1 cup drained and chopped Peppadews
4 pork sausages, casings removed
1 × 250g pack of streaky bacon

Preheat the oven to 180°C on the grill setting.

Start by butterflying the pork fillet. Remove the silver skin. Holding a sharp knife lengthwise, cut through the length of the fillet, making sure not to cut right through. Then, open up the pork fillet and press down gently to flatten it out.

In a bowl, mix together the chilli, onion, baby spinach, Peppadews and pork sausage meat until well combined. Spread the mixture over one half of the butterflied pork fillet and fold over the other half to close. Wrap the entire fillet with rashers of streaky bacon. Place the stuffed fillet on an oven tray, and grill in the oven for 45 minutes, or until golden brown in colour. Serve with Hollandaise Sauce (see p. 126).

GLAZED PORK BELLY

SERVES 6

1 kg pork belly
1 medium onion, finely chopped
½ cup apricot jam
⅓ cup Worcestershire sauce
4 cloves garlic, finely chopped
2 Tbsp grated ginger
2 red chillies, seeds removed, and finely chopped
½ cup white grape vinegar
½ cup apple cider vinegar
1 Tbsp chicken spice
1 tsp paprika

Preheat the oven to 180°C.

To a large pot, add the pork belly and onion. Cover with water, bring to a boil, and boil for 15–20 minutes. Drain and set aside.

In a saucepan over low heat, mix the apricot jam, Worcestershire sauce, garlic, ginger, red chillies, white vinegar, apple cider vinegar, chicken spice and paprika. Cook until the glaze has reduced and thickened.

Transfer the pork belly to a roasting dish. Use a sharp knife to remove the skin. Score the fat with the knife, then transfer to the oven and roast for 45–60 minutes, or until the pork is cooked through, and the fat is crispy and golden brown. Remove from the oven and pour over half the glaze, before transferring to the oven to roast for another 10 minutes. Pour over the remaining glaze and garnish as desired before serving.

CHICKEN

LEMON AND HERB BUTTERFLIED CHICKEN

SERVES 6–8

1 whole chicken (± 1.2kg), gizzards removed
Salt and pepper, to taste
½ cup plain yoghurt
¼ cup olive oil
¼ cup lemon juice
Handful finely chopped fresh coriander, plus extra sprigs to garnish
Handful finely chopped fresh parsley
½ cup finely chopped sundried tomatoes
4 cloves garlic, minced

Preheat the oven to 180°C on the grill setting.

First, butterfly the chicken. Place the chicken on the kitchen counter on its back. Using a sharp kitchen knife or kitchen scissors, cut open the breast. Turn over the chicken and, using the palm of your hand, press down on the back to flatten it. Place the chicken in a large roasting pan, and season with salt and pepper.

In a bowl, combine the yoghurt, olive oil, lemon juice, coriander, parsley, sundried tomatoes and garlic. Spread the mixture over the chicken, then cover the roasting pan with foil. Grill in the oven for 45 minutes. Remove the foil, return the chicken to the oven and grill for a further 10 minutes to brown. Garnish with coriander before serving.

CHICKEN AND RICE STIR-FRY

SERVES 3–4

2 chicken breast fillets, cut into strips
1 Tbsp chicken spice
2 Tbsp oil
1 onion, chopped
250g stir-fry vegetables (any kind will do)
¼ cup soy sauce
2 cups cooked long-grain white or brown rice
1 Tbsp spice for rice
Salt and pepper, to taste

Season the chicken with chicken spice and set aside.

In a pan, heat the oil over medium heat. Add the onion and fry until softened. Add the seasoned chicken strips, and fry for 3 minutes, or until browned. Stir through the stir-fry vegetables, soy sauce, rice and spice for rice. Mix well, season with salt and pepper, and cook for a further 4–6 minutes before serving.

CHICKEN AND MUSHROOM PIE

SERVES 3-4

1 Tbsp oil
1 medium onion, finely chopped
250g white button mushrooms, sliced
1 Tbsp finely chopped fresh thyme, plus extra sprigs to garnish
4 chicken breast fillets, cubed
1 Tbsp chicken spice
200ml chicken stock
1 cup fresh cream
Salt and pepper, to taste
1 × 400g roll frozen puff pastry, defrosted
1 egg, lightly beaten

Preheat the oven to 180°C.

Heat the oil in a pan over medium heat. Add the onion, mushrooms and thyme, then fry until soft. Add the chicken and chicken spice, and fry until the chicken is browned. Pour in the stock and cover the pan with a lid. Reduce the heat to low and simmer until the stock reduces and thickens. Pour in the cream, and season with salt and pepper. Continue to simmer until the sauce reduces and thickens.

Cut and shape the pastry to fit over a 30cm casserole dish. Spread the chicken and mushroom filling over the base of the casserole dish. Layer the sheet of pastry over the filling, trimming the edges if necessary. Cut a small slit in the centre to allow steam to escape while baking. Brush the pastry with the beaten egg. Bake the pie in the oven for 25–30 minutes, or until golden brown. Garnish with thyme sprigs before serving.

CHICKEN BREAST
COATED WITH COUSCOUS

I'm always thinking of new ways to elevate my dishes. Recently, I wanted to make crumbed chicken and I realised I didn't have any bread crumbs, but I spied the couscous in my pantry. The rest is history. Paired with Mustard-Mayo Coleslaw (see p. 98), it's perfect.

SERVES 2

- 1 cup uncooked couscous
- 1 Tbsp garlic powder
- 1 Tbsp chopped fresh thyme, plus extra sprigs to garnish
- 1 tsp cayenne pepper
- 1 Tbsp chicken spice
- 2 cups oil
- 2 chicken breast fillets
- 2 eggs, beaten

In a bowl, mix the couscous, garlic powder, thyme, cayenne pepper and chicken spice. Set aside.

In the meantime, heat the oil in a large saucepan over high heat.

Dip each chicken breast fillet in the beaten egg, then coat in the seasoned couscous mixture. Deep-fry the chicken fillets until cooked through and golden brown. Garnish with fresh thyme and serve with Mustard-Mayo Coleslaw (see p. 98)

GRILLED CHICKEN LEG QUARTERS

SERVES 4

4 chicken leg quarters
Salt and pepper, to taste
1 Tbsp chicken spice
1 Tbsp cayenne pepper
1 Tbsp wholegrain mustard
2 Tbsp chopped fresh thyme
2 Tbsp garlic flakes
1 Tbsp honey
3 Tbsp mayonnaise
2 Tbsp lemon juice

Arrange the chicken portions in a roasting dish, and season with salt and pepper.

In a large bowl, combine the chicken spice, cayenne pepper, wholegrain mustard, thyme, garlic flakes, honey, mayonnaise and lemon juice. Pour this marinade over the chicken. Marinate for 1 hour or overnight.

Preheat the oven to 160°C on the convection setting (with upper and lower elements on), unless marinating overnight.

Place the chicken in the oven, then grill, uncovered, for 45 minutes, turning every 10 minutes to ensure it cooks evenly. Serve garnished as desired.

SEAFOOD

SALMON
WITH LEMON BUTTER SAUCE AND TOASTED ALMOND FLAKES

SERVES 3

3 × 150g salmon steaks
1 Tbsp fish spice
1 Tbsp oil
60g flaked almonds, toasted

FOR THE SAUCE

60g butter
2 cloves garlic, crushed
100ml fresh cream
1 Tbsp lemon juice
Salt and pepper, to taste

Season the salmon steaks with the fish spice. Heat the oil in a frying pan over high heat, and fry the salmon steaks for 3–4 minutes per side. Remove from the pan and set aside.

To make the sauce, lower the heat. Melt the butter and sauté the garlic in the same pan for 1–2 minutes, or until fragrant. Add the fresh cream and lemon juice, and simmer for 2 minutes, or until the sauce has thickened. Season with salt and pepper. Pour the sauce over the salmon and sprinkle over the toasted almond flakes. Garnish as desired.

HAKE AND PRAWNS
IN A LEMON AND MUSTARD BUTTER SAUCE

SERVES 4

FOR THE HAKE AND PRAWNS

4 frozen hake fillets, defrosted
350g tiger prawns, deveined and sliced open
1 Tbsp garlic powder
1 Tbsp paprika
1 tsp salt
1 tsp ground black pepper
80g butter
2 cloves garlic, minced

FOR THE SAUCE

60g butter
2 cloves garlic, minced
½ cup dry white wine
1 Tbsp lemon juice
Handful finely chopped parsley
1 Tbsp English mustard
½ cup cream
Salt and pepper, to taste

Pat the hake and prawns dry with paper towel.

Mix together the garlic powder, paprika, salt and black pepper. Season the hake and prawns with the mixture.

Melt the butter in a nonstick pan over medium heat, then sauté the garlic for 1–2 minutes, or until fragrant. Add the seasoned hake and prawns and fry for 3 minutes. Remove from the pan and set aside.

To make the sauce, wipe the pan clean with paper towel. Add the butter to the pan and melt over low heat. Add the garlic, white wine, lemon juice, parsley and mustard, then stir in the cream. Season with salt and pepper, then simmer for 2 minutes, or until the sauce has reduced and has a smooth consistency.

Add the hake and prawns to the sauce, and stir to coat. Serve with lemon wedges.

ASIAN SEAFOOD FRIED RICE

SERVES 6–8

2 Tbsp oil
1 onion, diced
4 cloves garlic, minced
2 Tbsp grated ginger
1kg frozen mixed seafood (such as mussels, prawns, shrimp and calamari)
½ cup soy sauce
2 Tbsp rice vinegar
2–3 jalapeños, sliced
4 cups cooked basmati rice (cooked with 1 tsp ground turmeric)
Salt and pepper, to taste

Heat the oil in a pan over medium heat. Add the onion, garlic, ginger, mixed seafood, soy sauce, rice vinegar and jalapeños. Stir to mix, then cook for 10–12 minutes, until the liquid has reduced and the seafood is just cooked through. Stir through the rice, and season with salt and pepper. Serve hot.

DEEP-FRIED HAKE

SERVES 8

4 cups oil
2 cups cake wheat flour
1 Tbsp garlic powder
1 tsp paprika
2 Tbsp seafood seasoning
Salt and pepper, to taste
8 frozen hake fillets, defrosted
2 cups amasi
1 lemon, cut into wedges

Heat the oil over high heat in a deep saucepan.

In a wide, shallow bowl, combine the flour, garlic powder, paprika, seafood seasoning, and salt and pepper. Dip the hake fillets in the amasi, then dip them in the seasoned flour mixture, making sure they are coated on all sides.

Deep-fry the hake until the batter is golden, then remove and place on paper towel to absorb the excess oil. Serve with a squeeze of lemon juice and golden potato fries.

UMAMA WOMTHANDAZO
Woman of prayer

I'm from a very spiritual family, and my mom was a very prayerful woman. Growing up, I always saw abo Mama Bomthandazo as people who are very close to God and, being one of them, my mom motivated me to follow in her footsteps. I know I've touched many people when I'm in my church uniform. This is who I am and what I believe in. So, Sundays are my favourite days, because I get to spend time in church and cooking for my small family.

Most Sundays, I wake early, make breakfast for my husband and kids, and get a head start on lunch. I usually prepare and leave the roast in the oven on a low heat before I go to church. When we come home, we're welcomed by the warm aroma of a roast, and I'm already one step ahead, ready to start the salads and sides. I really recommend you find a rhythm to plan your Sunday lunch, too.

'So whether you eat or drink, or whatever you do, do all to the glory of God.'
(1 Corinthians 10:31)

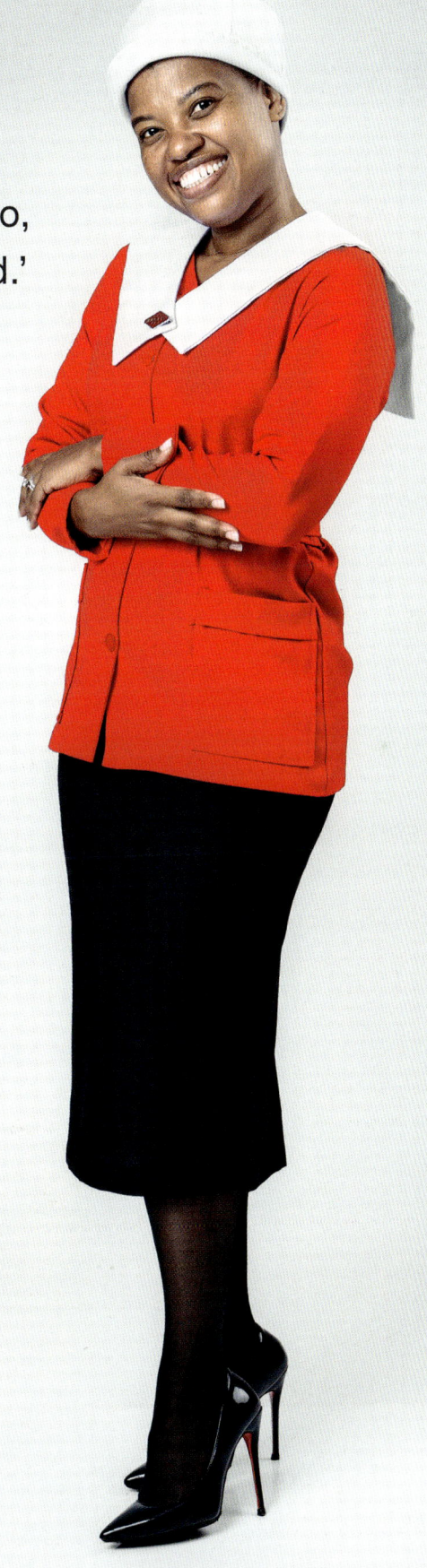

SUNDAY SPREAD

Everything tastes better on Sunday. Whether it's a simple butternut or a sumptuous roast, it's just a bit more special. Some call it Sunday kos, and some call it several colours or seven colours. One thing is for sure – this section is colourful and filled with many flavours. Let's tuck into our Sunday spread!

BACON-WRAPPED WHOLE CHICKEN

SERVES 6

1 whole chicken, gizzards removed
6–8 rashers streaky bacon
1 tsp dried mixed herbs
Salt and pepper, to taste
2 onions, quartered
8 cloves garlic
Sprigs fresh rosemary

Preheat the oven to 180°C.

Place the chicken in a roasting dish. Cover the breast area with the bacon, allowing the rashers to overlap. Scatter the dried mixed herbs over the entire chicken and season with salt and pepper. Stuff the onions, garlic and rosemary into the cavity.

Roast the chicken for 30 minutes, then remove from the oven and cover the dish with foil to prevent the chicken from drying out. Return to the oven and roast for a further 50–60 minutes, until the chicken is cooked through and the juices run clear.

Remove the chicken from the roasting dish and transfer to a serving plate. Leave to cool for 10 minutes before carving and serving.

ORANGE-CINNAMON ROASTED BUTTERNUT

SERVES 4

2 whole unpeeled medium butternuts, cut into wedges and seeds removed
Salt and pepper, to taste
¼ cup melted butter
1 Tbsp ground cinnamon
2–3 Tbsp white sugar
Juice of 1 orange or ½ cup orange juice

Preheat the oven to 180°C.

Arrange the butternut wedges on a baking tray and season with salt and pepper.

In a bowl, mix together the melted butter, cinnamon, sugar and orange juice. Use a spoon to drizzle the glaze over the butternut. Roast in the oven for 50–60 minutes, or until golden brown.

MUSTARD-MAYO COLESLAW

Whether it's a wedding, family gathering or Christmas lunch, coleslaw will surely be on the menu. This is one famous salad, and I doubt it will ever go out of fashion. We all love coleslaw, so it has to be part of our Sunday spread, but this time with a twist!

SERVES 4

FOR THE COLESLAW
3 cups shredded white cabbage
1 cup grated carrot
½ cup raisins
1 large red onion, thinly sliced
Handful fresh dill, chives, parsley or coriander, finely chopped (optional)

FOR THE DRESSING
1 Tbsp English mustard
100ml mayonnaise
100ml plain yoghurt or sour cream
2 Tbsp honey
Salt and pepper, to taste

In a bowl, combine the shredded cabbage, grated carrot, raisins, sliced onion and herbs (if using).

In a separate small bowl, mix together the dressing ingredients. Pour the dressing over the salad and toss until well coated.

BEETROOT, FETA AND PINE NUT SALAD

SERVES 6

6 whole beetroot, peeled and diced
1 Tbsp vinegar or lemon juice
200g rocket leaves
4 seedless naartjies, peeled and segmented
1 cup crumbled feta cheese
1 Tbsp roasted pine nuts

FOR THE DRESSING

¼ cup white balsamic vinegar
¼ cup olive oil
Handful fresh mint, finely chopped
Salt and pepper, to taste

Add the beetroot to a large pot and cover with 4 cups of water. Pour in the vinegar or lemon juice (see Tip) and bring to a boil. Boil for 20 minutes, or until the beetroot is soft.

Arrange the rocket on the bottom of a salad bowl. Layer the beetroot on top, followed by the naartjie segments, feta cheese and pine nuts.

To make the dressing, mix together all the ingredients in a small bowl. Drizzle over the salad just before serving.

TIP

Do not toss this salad, as the beetroot will discolour the rest of the ingredients, leaving you with a messy-looking salad.

Adding vinegar or lemon juice to the boiling water prevents the beetroot from 'bleeding'.

SUNDAY SPREAD

SAVOURY RICE

SERVES 4

2 Tbsp oil
1 small onion, chopped
1 red pepper, pith removed, and chopped
1 Tbsp ground cumin
1 Tbsp ground coriander
1 tsp smoked paprika
500g lean beef mince
1 × 410g can black beans, drained
2 cups cooked long-grain white rice
Salt and pepper, to taste

Heat the oil in a pan over medium heat. Add the onion, red pepper, cumin, coriander and paprika, and fry for 2 minutes. Add the mince, breaking it up with a fork, and cook until browned. Using a fork, gently stir in the beans and rice, then season with salt and pepper, and serve.

CREAMY SPINACH AND MUSHROOMS

SERVES 4

2 Tbsp oil
1 small onion, chopped
2 cloves garlic, minced
300g sliced white button mushrooms
1kg baby spinach
½ cup drained and chopped Peppadews
1 × 250g tub plain cream cheese
Salt and pepper, to taste

In a pan, heat the oil over medium heat. Add the onion, garlic and mushrooms, and sauté for 2 minutes, or until softened. Mix in the baby spinach and Peppadews, then stir in the cream cheese until the consistency becomes thick. Season with salt and pepper.

Savoury Rice

Creamy Spinach and Mushrooms

ROASTED BABY HAKE

SERVES 4

800g whole frozen baby hake (skin on), defrosted
1 Tbsp fish spice
1 tsp paprika
2 cloves garlic, minced
1 Tbsp chopped fresh coriander
100ml melted butter or margarine
100ml lemon juice
Lemon wedges, to garnish

Preheat the oven to 180°C.

Using a sharp knife, cut slits into the flesh of the fish. Place the fish in an oven dish.

In a bowl, mix together the fish spice, paprika, garlic, fresh coriander, melted butter or margarine, and lemon juice. Drizzle the mixture over the baby hake and roast for 20 minutes, or until firm but moist. Garnish as desired and serve with lemon wedges.

ROAST BEEF AND VEGETABLES

There is no Sunday without a roast. I think roasts are the easiest dishes to prepare because you marinate and then leave the oven do all the work. So, on Sundays the roast is always my go-to dish.

SERVES 6

1.5kg beef roast
Salt and pepper, to taste
2 cloves garlic, minced
1 Tbsp brown sugar
1 Tbsp dried thyme
¼ cup Worcestershire sauce
1 tsp olive oil
¼ cup tomato paste
2 medium red onions, quartered
300g baby potatoes
250g baby carrots
2 red peppers, pith removed, and roughly chopped
1 yellow pepper, pith removed, and roughly chopped

Preheat the oven to 180°C.

Season the beef roast all over with salt and pepper. Set aside.

In a small bowl, mix together the garlic, brown sugar, dried thyme, Worcestershire sauce, olive oil and tomato paste. Rub the mixture all over the beef.

Place the beef in a roasting dish and cover with foil. Roast in the oven for 1 hour, then remove the foil and add the onions, potatoes, baby carrots and peppers to the dish. Cover again, return to the oven and roast for a further 30 minutes. Discard the foil and roast, uncovered, for another 15 minutes, until golden brown.

GREEN BEAN AND BACON POTATO SALAD

SERVES 6

250g baby potatoes, boiled
200g green beans, ends trimmed, and blanched (see p. 31 for how to blanch vegetables)
½ cup cooked chopped bacon
½ red onion, thinly sliced
2 Tbsp chopped fresh chives

FOR THE DRESSING

1 clove garlic, minced
½ cup olive oil
2 Tbsp honey
3–4 Tbsp English mustard
¼ cup balsamic vinegar
Salt and pepper, to taste

Cut the cooked baby potatoes into halves. Add them to a salad bowl, along with the blanched green beans, bacon, onion and chives.

In a separate, small bowl, mix together the garlic, olive oil, honey, English mustard and balsamic vinegar. Season with salt and pepper. Pour the dressing over the salad and mix until well coated.

HOME GROWN

I'm fourth-born of the late Mjombo and Nomsa Hadebe. My parents named me Zanele, which means 'enough', because they were sure I'd be the last of their daughters. Little did they know there would still be another two! I grew up with many siblings – five sisters and a brother – in a small village where all we had was one another. Yet, we were a happy family, thanks to umah who taught us unity: 'Noma sengifile bantabami nihlale nazi angeke ngikujabulela ukunibona ningazwani ('You guys must stick together, even when I'm gone').'

Food was something that kept our family together. From as early as I can remember, family life revolved around meals. In the evenings, we would make a fire in a rondavel. We'd all sit around it while umah made a simple potato curry and uphuthu, or, if we were lucky, her famous bone marrow and ujeqe.

Sometimes, my sisters and I would take turns to cook, although, I can't really remember if I enjoyed cooking back then. Mama always wanted food on the stove or umdoko. She taught us that food keeps the home warm, saying, 'If someone comes by, what are you going to feed them?' Now you know the importance and origin of 'senidlile kodwa' for me.

Home is always where my heart is.

INKUKHU YASE KHAYA
WITH A TWIST
(HARDBODY CHICKEN)

Some call it a free-range chicken, others name it hardbody. I saw a comment on social media that isiZulu-speaking people who call this chicken 'inkukhu yesiZulu' sound as though they conversed with the chicken in isiZulu and it responded in isiZulu. Hahaha, I really find that funny. Well, we call it that, but all in all it's a chicken that roams around the yard. Mostly, we get to eat one on special occasions. For instance, if we did well at school we would get a chicken slaughtered as a reward on Sunday for lunch. Normally it's cooked with onion and a stock, but this recipe has a Zanele twist. I hope you love it.

SERVES 6–8

- 1 Tbsp oil
- 1 umleqwa (hardbody chicken), cut into 8 portions
- 1 onion, diced
- 3 cloves garlic, minced
- 4 sprigs fresh thyme
- 1 Tbsp mild curry powder
- 1 Tbsp ground cumin
- 3 cups chicken stock
- 1 green pepper, pith removed, and chopped
- 1 red pepper, pith removed, and chopped
- Salt and pepper, to taste

In a large pot, heat the oil over medium heat. Add the chicken portions, fry until browned, then remove from the pot and set aside.

In the same pot, fry the onion, garlic, thyme, curry powder and cumin until fragrant. Return the chicken to the pot, pour in the stock and simmer, covered, for 1 hour over medium heat, topping up with more stock or water if the stock reduces too much.

Add the green and red peppers, season with salt and pepper, and cook for a further 20 minutes, until the liquid has reduced and thickened into a sauce.

SAMP AND BEANS

SERVES 10

3–4 cups uncooked samp and beans mix, rinsed thoroughly, and soaked overnight
1 Tbsp oil
1 large onion, diced
1 Tbsp hot curry powder
1 Tbsp steak and chops spice
1 green pepper, pith removed, and chopped
2 cups beef stock

Drain the samp and beans mix. Add it to a large pot and cover with clean water. Leave it to simmer slowly over low heat until nearly soft, stirring frequently. Check it every 30 minutes and add more water, if necessary. Once cooked, remove the samp and beans from the heat and drain off any remaining water.

In a separate pot, heat the oil over medium heat and fry the onion until soft. Add the curry powder and steak and chops spice. Fry for 1 minute, stirring continuously. Add the cooked samp and beans, and the beef stock, then simmer slowly until the liquid has evaporated, stirring occasionally. The samp and beans should have a nice creamy, soft texture. Garnish as desired.

UJEQE
(STEAMED BREAD)

This is my mom's speciality. We always knew it was a good day when mom made ujeqe! To this day, when I go home, I place an order with her, because no one makes ujeqe better than my mom. She always mixes the flour with maize meal, because she believes in saving flour! I would love to believe I learnt from her because mine is just as nice – but not better than hers. I love you, Mah!

SERVES 6

4 cups cake wheat flour
1 tsp salt
2 tsp sugar
10g instant dry yeast
600ml warm water, plus more, if necessary

Combine the flour, salt, sugar and yeast in a large bowl. Using your hands, make a well in the centre and add the water – enough to make a dough. Knead for 8–10 minutes, until the dough is smooth and elastic. If the dough is still too dry, slowly add more water as needed.

Transfer the dough to a greased bowl and cover with cling wrap or a kitchen towel. Leave in a warm place for 30 minutes to rise until doubled in size.

Once it has risen, knock down the dough (punch it gently using your fist) to release the larger air bubbles, and cut it into 6 equal pieces. Place each piece in its own ramekin.

Place the ramekins in a big pot. Fill the pot with just enough water to reach halfway up the ramekins. You need enough water to gently steam the dough, but not too much that when it boils it covers and wets the dough. Steam for 20–25 minutes, or until a toothpick inserted into the centre comes out clean.

HERBED BEEF TRIPE

SERVES 4

1kg beef tripe
2 Tbsp oil
1 large onion, chopped
4 cloves garlic, minced
3 Tbsp chopped fresh rosemary and thyme
Salt and pepper, to taste
4 cups beef stock
Sliced spring onion, to garnish

In a pot, add the tripe and cover with water. On medium heat, boil the tripe for 90 minutes, adding more water if necessary, until soft. Once cooked, drain and set aside.

Heat the oil in a pot over medium heat. Add the onion, garlic, rosemary and thyme, cooked tripe, salt and pepper, and stock. Cook for 8–12 minutes, until the stock has reduced and thickened to a sauce. Garnish with sliced spring onion.

UPHUTHU NE KLABISHI
(UPHUTHU AND CABBAGE)

This is a famous meal in my village and is referred to as 'intombi yesigodi' (local girl). It's not just an affordable meal, but one that fills the soul. When I eat it, it always takes me home to my mom's rondavel, wherever I am.

SERVES 6

FOR THE UPHUTHU
4 cups water
2 cups maize meal
1 tsp salt

FOR THE CABBAGE
1 Tbsp oil
1 onion, chopped
4–6 rashers streaky bacon, chopped (optional)
1 Tbsp mild curry powder
½ head green cabbage, roughly chopped
1 cup chopped mixed red, green and yellow peppers
Salt and pepper, to taste

In a pot, bring the water to a boil. Add the maize meal and salt in a heap in the centre of the pot. Lower the heat. Using a fork, mix the maize meal, salt and water until a crumbly mixture forms. Close the lid and cook for 25 minutes, stirring every 5 minutes. Remove from the heat

Heat the oil in a pan over medium heat. Add the onion and sauté for 2 minutes, or until lightly golden. Add the bacon and stir until cooked. Mix in the curry powder, then stir in the cabbage and peppers. Cook over low heat until the cabbage is soft. Season with salt and pepper. Serve alongside the uphuthu.

ELEVATE YOUR MEAL:
SAUCES, DRESSINGS DIPS & MARINADES

As they say, the secret is in the sauce! I believe the sauce marks the start of a beautiful dish. Let's make our own! I love that you can double or triple these recipes and freeze the leftovers for later use.

SAUCES

Hollandaise Sauce

Creamy Peppercorn Sauce

HOLLANDAISE SAUCE

This is the sauce that makes Eggs Benedict my favourite. It's also often served on blanched vegetables and seafood. I'm not shy to admit that I prefer my hollandaise, so I hope you do, too.

SERVES 2

- 2 egg yolks
- 2 Tbsp lemon juice
- 3 Tbsp white spirit vinegar
- ½ cup melted butter
- Salt and pepper, to taste

Place the egg yolks in a heatproof bowl, then place the bowl over a pot of simmering water. Using a whisk, mix the egg yolks until they start to become runny. While whisking, pour in the lemon juice and vinegar, then add the melted butter. Keep whisking (but be careful not to overmix), until the sauce becomes thick and creamy. Season with salt and pepper.

CREAMY PEPPERCORN SAUCE

SERVES 4

- 15g butter
- 2 cloves garlic, minced
- 1 cup fresh cream
- ¼ cup brandy
- 2 Tbsp whole black peppercorns
- 1 tsp salt
- 100ml milk
- 1 tsp cake wheat flour

In a saucepan, melt the butter over medium heat. Add the garlic and sauté for 1–2 minutes, or until fragrant. Pour in the cream and brandy, and add the peppercorns and salt. Simmer for 2 minutes.

In a cup, use a fork to mix the milk and flour. Add the mixture to the sauce and simmer for 2–3 minutes, or until thickened.

CHIMICHURRI

SERVES 4

1 red onion, finely chopped
Handful fresh parsley, finely chopped
Handful fresh mint, finely chopped
2 red chillies, seeds removed, and finely chopped
¼ cup olive oil
¼ cup apple cider vinegar
Salt and pepper, to taste

Add all the ingredients to a bowl and mix until well combined.

MUSTARD SAUCE

SERVES 4

½ cup mayonnaise
3 Tbsp Dijon mustard
1 Tbsp wholegrain mustard
½ cup white spirit vinegar
1 tsp cayenne pepper
Salt and pepper, to taste

Add all the ingredients to a bowl and mix until well combined.

BLUE CHEESE SAUCE

SERVES 4

30g butter
1 clove garlic, minced
1 cup fresh cream
½ cup crumbled blue cheese
¼ cup milk
5ml cornflour
1 Tbsp dried parsley
Salt and pepper, to taste

In a saucepan over low heat, melt the butter, then add the garlic, cream and blue cheese, and mix well. Let it simmer. Combine the milk and cornflour in a jug, and pour into the pan (to thicken the sauce). Sprinkle in dried parsley, salt and pepper.

DRESSINGS

No one likes a dry salad. Well, I don't!
The dressing always elevates the salad and adds extra flavour.
So why not? Let's take our salads to new heights!

WHOLEGRAIN MUSTARD DRESSING

SERVES 4

2 Tbsp wholegrain mustard
1 Tbsp English mustard
2 Tbsp honey
100ml white wine vinegar
100ml olive oil
Salt and pepper, to taste

Add all the ingredients to a bowl and mix until combined.

ASIAN SESAME DRESSING

SERVES 4

½ cup rice vinegar
2 Tbsp olive oil
2 Tbsp soya sauce
1 Tbsp toasted sesame seeds
1 Tbsp grated ginger
3 Tbsp sesame oil

Add all the ingredients to a bowl and mix until combined.

CREAMY BLUE CHEESE DRESSING

SERVES 6

½ cup mayonnaise
200g crumbled blue cheese
2 Tbsp lemon juice
1 Tbsp chopped fresh parsley
¼ cup sour cream
Salt and pepper, to taste

To the jug of a blender, add all the ingredients and blend until well combined and creamy.

DIPS

Dips are the perfect bowls filled with flavours – great for sharing! I love hosting, and snacks and cheese boards are a winner if you are having a group of people over. Let's just dip in!

Feta Cheese Dip

Hummus

CREAMY BLUE CHEESE DRESSING

SERVES 6

½ cup mayonnaise
200g crumbled blue cheese
2 Tbsp lemon juice
1 Tbsp chopped fresh parsley
¼ cup sour cream
Salt and pepper, to taste

To the jug of a blender, add all the ingredients and blend until well combined and creamy.

DIPS

Dips are the perfect bowls filled with flavours – great for sharing! I love hosting, and snacks and cheese boards are a winner if you are having a group of people over. Let's just dip in!

Feta Cheese Dip

Hummus

HUMMUS

SERVES 8

1 × 410g can chickpeas
2 cloves garlic, minced
3–4 Tbsp lemon juice
1 tsp ground cumin
½ tsp salt
2 Tbsp olive oil, plus extra to drizzle
1 tsp paprika

Drain the chickpeas into a bowl, reserving half the liquid. Rinse the chickpeas, then place them in the jug of a blender, making sure to reserve a few to use as garnish later. Add the garlic, lemon juice, cumin, salt and the reserved chickpea liquid. Switch on the blender and, with the motor running on low (to avoid splatter), drizzle in the olive oil. Blend until the mixture is smooth, thick and creamy.

Transfer the hummus to a dipping bowl. Sprinkle with the paprika and a drizzle of olive oil. Garnish with the reserved chickpeas.

TZATZIKI DIP

SERVES 8

1 small cucumber
1 cup plain yoghurt
2 cloves garlic, minced
Salt and pepper, to taste

Cut the cucumber in half lengthways and scoop out the seeds. Grate the cucumber into a bowl, then squeeze it in your hands to drain off excess water (see Tip).

Mix the grated cucumber with the yoghurt and garlic, and season with salt and pepper.

> **NOTE**
> Squeezing out the excess water will prevent the tzatziki from becoming too watery.

JALAPEÑO DIP

SERVES 4

1 × 250g tub plain cream cheese
½ cup finely chopped pickled jalapeño
2 cloves garlic, minced
1 Tbsp dried chilli flakes
½ cup mayonnaise

Add all the ingredients to a bowl and mix until combined.

FETA CHEESE DIP

SERVES 8

200g plain feta cheese
1 × 250g tub plain cream cheese
Freshly squeezed juice of 2 lemons
2 Tbsp honey
Handful fresh dill
1 cup roasted pine nuts (optional)

Add all the ingredients to the jug of a blender and blend until smooth.

GUACAMOLE

SERVES 4

1 ripe avocado
¼ cup cream cheese
Squeeze of lemon juice
Salt and pepper, to taste

In a bowl, mash the avocado and cream cheese together. Add the lemon juice, season with salt and pepper, and mix well.

ELEVATE YOUR MEAL

MARINADES

*At the beginning of my food journey,
I didn't know one could actually make homemade marinades.
When I realised that I could make my own from scratch,
it was really fulfilling. I hope you experience the same
satisfaction I had after trying these. Enjoy!*

*Lemon and Herb
Marinade*

PREGO MARINADE

This marinade is best used with chicken or steak.

SERVES 4

30g butter
2 Tbsp olive oil
4 cloves garlic, minced
4 red or green chillies, finely chopped
1 Tbsp paprika
1 tsp mild curry powder
½ cup plain yoghurt
100ml lemon juice
Salt and pepper, to taste

Melt the butter in a pan over low heat and add the olive oil. Sauté the garlic until fragrant, then stir in the chillies, paprika, curry powder, plain yoghurt, lemon juice, and salt and pepper. Simmer for 3–5 minutes, until smooth.

If not using immediately, allow to cool, pour into a Ziploc bag or freezer-safe container and store in the freezer for up to 3 months.

YOGHURT AND MINT MARINADE

This is great to marinate seafood, chicken or lamb.

SERVES 6

1 cup plain yoghurt
100ml olive oil
4 cloves garlic, minced
Handful fresh ginger, finely chopped
Handful fresh mint, finely chopped
Salt and pepper, to taste

Add all the ingredients to a bowl and mix to combine.

If not using immediately, allow to cool, pour into a Ziploc bag or freezer-safe container and store in the freezer for up to 3 months.

BALSAMIC VINEGAR MARINADE

This marinade pairs very well with any red meat, pork and vegetables.

SERVES 4

20g butter
4 tsp olive oil
2 cloves garlic, minced
½ cup balsamic vinegar
100ml water
2 Tbsp brown sugar
1 Tbsp dried chilli flakes
1 Tbsp finely chopped rosemary
Salt and pepper, to taste

Melt the butter in a pan over low heat. Add the olive oil and garlic, and sauté until fragrant. Pour in the balsamic vinegar, water and sugar. Stir in the chilli flakes and rosemary, and season with salt and pepper. Simmer for 3–5 minutes, or until reduced.

If not using immediately, allow to cool, pour into a Ziploc bag or freezer-safe container and store in the freezer for up to 3 months.

LEMON AND HERB MARINADE

This marinade is especially delicious with chicken or fish.

SERVES 4

½ cup olive oil
½ cup lemon juice
1 Tbsp finely chopped fresh parsley
1 Tbsp finely chopped fresh rosemary
1 Tbsp finely chopped fresh thyme
2 cloves garlic, minced
Salt and pepper, to taste

Add all the ingredients to a bowl and mix until combined.

If not using immediately, allow to cool, pour into a Ziploc bag or freezer-safe container and store in the freezer for up to 3 months.

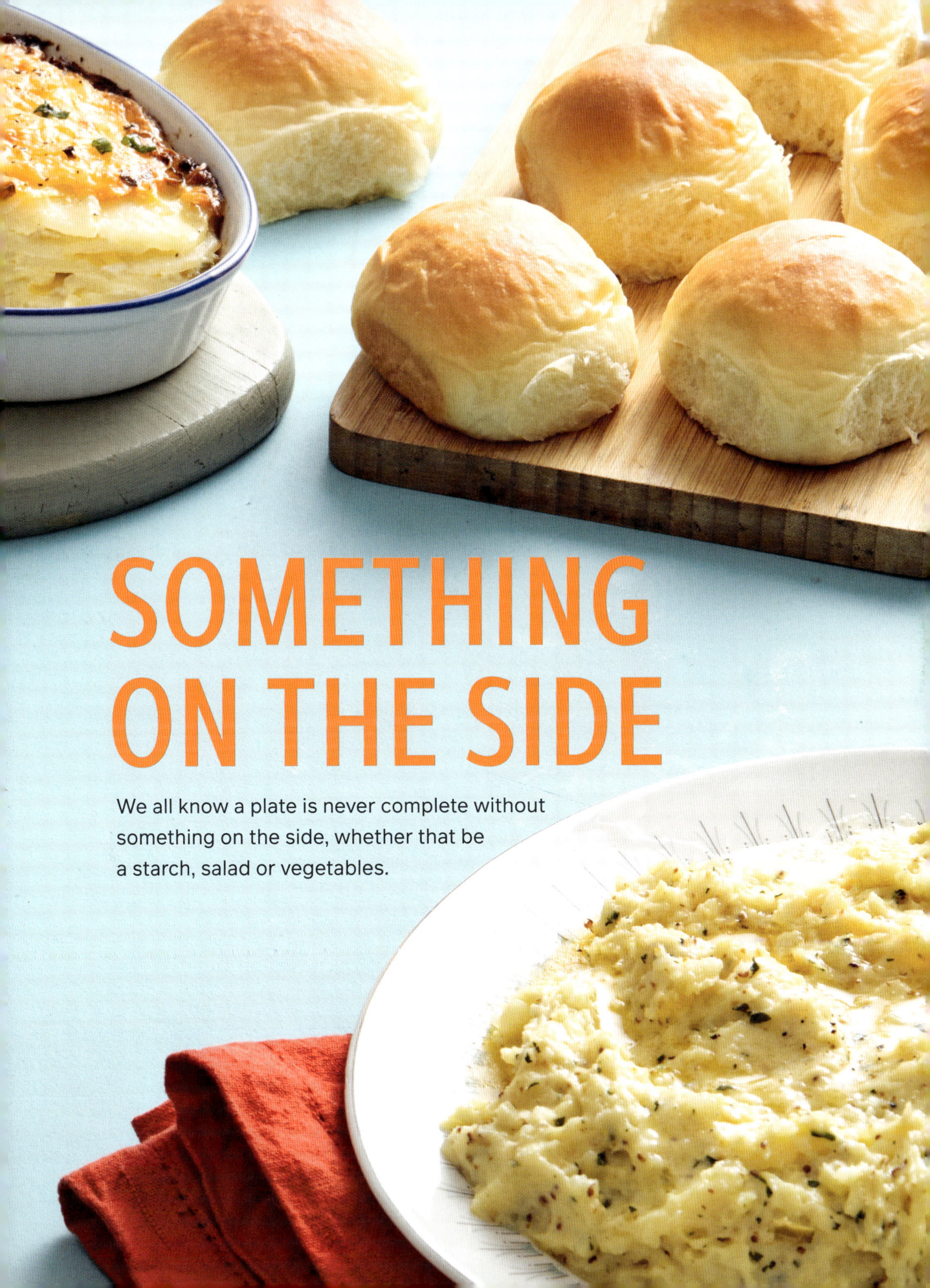

SOMETHING ON THE SIDE

We all know a plate is never complete without something on the side, whether that be a starch, salad or vegetables.

CHEESY-MUSTARD MASHED POTATOES

SERVES 4

6 large potatoes, peeled and cubed
2 cloves garlic, peeled
60g butter or good quality margarine
1 Tbsp wholegrain mustard
3 Tbsp English mustard
2 cups fresh cream
50g grated mozzarella cheese
Salt and pepper, to taste
Handful fresh parsley, finely chopped

Boil the potatoes along with the garlic in salted water until the potatoes are soft. Drain the excess water from the pot. Add the butter or margarine, wholegrain mustard and English mustard. Mash the potatoes using a potato masher, pouring in the cream as you do so. Stir in the grated mozzarella. When all the ingredients are combined and the mixture is smooth and creamy, season with salt and pepper, and mix in the fresh parsley.

POTATO BAKE

SERVES 4

4 medium–large potatoes, peeled, rinsed and thinly sliced
2 cups fresh cream, divided
Salt and pepper, to taste
2 cups chopped spring onions, divided
¾ cup grated cheese of your choice

Preheat the oven to 180°C.

Layer half the sliced potatoes at the bottom of a large, shallow baking dish, allowing them to overlap. Pour over 1 cup of cream to cover, and season with salt and pepper. Spread over 1 cup of the spring onions. Repeat, and season again.

Top with the cheese and cover with a lid or foil. If the dish is very full, place a rimmed baking tray underneath. Bake for 1 hour. Remove the lid or foil and bake for a further 30 minutes, until the top is golden brown.

CREAMY SAMP
WITH MUSHROOMS

Samp is one of my mom's specialities; she likes to mix it with beans. I love to give my mom's recipes a twist, but she thinks she still does it better. I can't disagree with her.

SERVES 6

- 1½ cups uncooked samp
- 1 tsp olive or canola oil
- 1 onion, chopped
- 1 tsp minced garlic
- 1 cup sliced brown mushrooms
- Salt and pepper, to taste
- 30g butter
- 1 × 250g tub cream cheese
- ½ cup chopped chives

Soak the samp overnight, then drain. Add to a pot and cover with water. Bring to a boil, then cook over medium heat until soft.

In a separate pot, heat the oil over medium heat. Add the onion and garlic, and sauté until fragrant. Add the mushrooms and cook until softened, then add the cooked samp and stir. Season with salt and pepper, then stir in the butter and cream cheese. Turn off the heat and sprinkle in the chopped chives.

MANGO ATCHAAR

SERVES 8

- 3–4 hard green mangoes, peeled, pits removed, and cubed
- 6 cloves garlic, roughly chopped
- 5 Tbsp atchaar/pickle masala
- 3 Tbsp mustard seeds
- 1 Tbsp salt
- ¼ cup red chilli powder
- ½ cup white spirit vinegar
- 2 cups oil

In a bowl, mix all the ingredients together. Transfer the mixture to a 1-litre clean glass jar or plastic container. Cover the atchaar with the oil. Refrigerate in an airtight container for a few days, then stir the atchaar gently to mix. The atchaar is then ready to enjoy!

Creamy Samp with Mushrooms

Cheesy-Mustard Mashed Potatoes

Potato Bake

SOFT BREAD ROLLS

*These are always my go-to, either as a side or main.
I love that I can enjoy them just with butter and off I go.*

MAKES 12

1 cup lukewarm milk
½ cup sugar
10g instant dry yeast
100ml melted butter, plus extra for brushing
4 cups cake wheat flour
1 tsp salt

To a mixing bowl, add the milk, sugar and yeast. Mix well, then let it rest for about 12 minutes, or until bubbles form. Stir in the melted butter, then gradually mix in the flour, a little at a time. Add the salt and mix until the dough comes together. Cover with cling wrap or kitchen towel, and leave to rest until doubled in size.

Once doubled in size, divide the dough into golf ball-sized balls. Place the balls of dough on a greased baking tray, leaving space in-between for rising. Set aside to rest for another 30 minutes, or until doubled in size. Meanwhile, preheat the oven to 160°C.

Bake for 23–25 minutes, or until a toothpick inserted into the centre comes out clean.

To give the rolls a glossy finish, brush the tops with melted butter as soon as they come out of the oven.

BACON AND PEPPER PASTA SALAD

SERVES 2-4

2 cups cooked farfalle pasta
1 red pepper, pith removed, and finely chopped
1 yellow pepper, pith removed, and finely chopped
1 cup cooked chopped bacon
1 small red onion, thinly sliced
Handful chopped fresh parsley
Salt and pepper, to taste

FOR THE DRESSING

½ cup mayonnaise
½ cup basil pesto
100ml balsamic vinegar
100ml honey

In a large bowl, combine the cooked pasta, peppers, bacon, onion and parsley. Season to taste.

To make the dressing, in a small bowl or jug, mix together the mayonnaise, pesto, balsamic vinegar and honey until well combined. Pour over the dressing just before serving, and stir through the pasta until well coated. Season with more salt and pepper, if needed.

GOOD FOOD TASTES BETTER WHEN IT'S SHARED WITH FRIENDS

Food is a lifestyle. It has a way of bringing people together, from strangers to friends. My friends and I love nibbles. We always have a cheese board or some platters around when we have our get-togethers. And, given what I do for a living, they like to take chances by expecting me to cook for them at our get-togethers! Hahaha!

Well, they certainly love my chicken wings (see p. 158 for some Spiced-up Chicken Wings), which are always my go-to when we meet up.

Food is a huge part of my life, but life is also better with friends. My friends supported me through my transition from the corporate to culinary world, and were always there to celebrate with me. Thank you to my girls for understanding me, and for always holding my hand through the good and bad times.

NIBBLES

Come, let's have a bite! These quick-fix recipes are easy to prepare and always leave your taste buds wanting more. These nibbles make great starters, are handy for picnics or, if you're having friends over, for a get-together.

MOZZARELLA AND BACON RICE BALLS

MAKES 8–12

2 cups cooked long-grain rice
4 eggs, divided
1 cup cooked diced bacon
1 Tbsp dried thyme
1 Tbsp vegetable seasoning
200g mozzarella cheese, cut into cubes
1 cup breadcrumbs
4 cups oil

In a bowl, mix together the rice, 2 eggs, bacon, thyme and vegetable seasoning until well combined. Shape the mixture into golf ball-sized balls. Press a hole into the centre of each ball and stuff it with a cube of mozzarella. Roll the ball between your palms to enclose the mozzarella in the rice mixture.

Lightly whisk the remaining 2 eggs. Dip each rice ball in the egg and then coat in the breadcrumbs.

Add the oil to a pot and heat over high heat. Deep-fry the balls in the hot oil (see Tip) for 3–5 minutes, or until golden brown. Garnish as desired before serving.

TIP It's very important that the oil is hot enough for frying, otherwise the rice balls will turn out soggy. A quick and easy way to test if the oil is hot enough is to place a grain of uncooked rice in the hot oil. If it rises to the surface and starts to pop and fry, the oil should be ready for frying.

Spiced-up Chicken Wings

Tandoori Grilled Chicken Wings

SPICED-UP CHICKEN WINGS

SERVES 4

12 chicken wings
4 cups oil
1 cup cake wheat flour
3 Tbsp chicken spice
1 Tbsp dried mixed herbs
1 Tbsp ground ginger

FOR THE SAUCE

30g butter
2 gloves garlic, minced
2 Tbsp brown sugar
1 Tbsp paprika
1 Tbsp dried chilli flakes
½ cup plain yoghurt
½ cup lemon juice
3 fresh red chillies, seeds removed, and chopped (optional)
Salt and pepper, to taste

Cut the chicken wings into 3 pieces – the wingette, the drumette and the wing tip. Discard the wing tips, and set aside the wingettes and drumettes.

Heat the oil in a pan over high heat.

In the meantime, in a bowl, mix the flour, chicken spice, dried mixed herbs and ground ginger. Dip the chicken pieces in the mixture, making sure they are coated all over. Then, deep-fry the chicken pieces for 8–10 minutes, until cooked through and golden. Remove from the oil and transfer to a plate lined with paper towel. Set aside.

To make the sauce, melt the butter in a pan over medium heat. Add the garlic, sugar, paprika, dried chilli flakes, yoghurt, lemon juice, chillies, and salt and pepper. Simmer for 5–6 minutes, until the sauce is smooth, then remove from the heat. Place the wings in the sauce and stir to coat.

TANDOORI GRILLED CHICKEN WINGS

I love Indian cuisine. I love the spices, the aroma, the strong taste... I just love spicy food. However, sometimes I have to compromise on the heat when I cook so my little ones can enjoy the food with us.

SERVES 4

½ cup plain yoghurt
⅓ cup lemon juice
¼ cup olive oil
1 Tbsp ground cumin
1 Tbsp dried chilli flakes
1 Tbsp paprika
1 Tbsp dried mixed herbs
Salt and pepper, to taste
8–12 chicken wings

Prepare a braai, or preheat the oven to 180°C.

In a bowl, mix together the yoghurt, lemon juice, olive oil, ground cumin, dried chilli flakes, paprika and dried mixed herbs. Season with salt and pepper. Pour the marinade over the chicken wings, making sure they are coated all over. Marinate for 1 hour or overnight.

Flame-grill the wings over an open fire, until cooked through. Alternatively, grill the wings in the oven for 25–30 minutes, or until cooked through.

SUPER-EASY CHICKEN AND BACON BITES
WITH SWEET CHILLI SAUCE

Having friends over? Don't worry – I've got your back! These chicken and bacon bites are a life-saver, quick and easy yet very tasty.

SERVES 6

1 × 200g packet streaky bacon
2 large chicken breast fillets, trimmed and cut into cubes

FOR THE SWEET CHILLI SAUCE
30g butter
2 cloves garlic, minced
100g brown sugar
100ml lemon juice
2 Tbsp chicken spice
1 tsp cayenne pepper
2 fresh red chillies, seeds removed, and finely chopped

Preheat the oven to 180°C.

Cut the rashers of bacon in half. Wrap each cube of chicken with a half rasher of bacon, and fasten it in place with a toothpick or skewer. Place them on a baking tray and grill for 20 minutes, until the bacon is nice and crisp.

In the meantime, make the sweet chilli sauce. Melt the butter in a saucepan over low heat. Add the garlic and sauté for 30 seconds, or until fragrant. Stir in the brown sugar, lemon juice, chicken spice, cayenne pepper and chillies. Simmer until the sauce thickens, then transfer to a dipping bowl. To serve, dip the chicken and bacon bites in the sauce, and garnish as desired.

AVOCADO, PRAWN AND SALMON TOWER

SERVES 3

30g butter
2 cloves garlic, minced
6 prawns
4 Haas avocados
1 small red onion, finely chopped
2 Tbsp fresh dill, finely chopped
Juice of 1 lemon
Salt and pepper, to taste
1 cup chopped smoked salmon
Handful of micro herbs, to garnish

In a pan over medium heat, melt the butter. Add the garlic and sauté until fragrant. Add the prawns and fry for 2 minutes on each side, or until they turn pinkish in colour.

To a mixing bowl, add the flesh of the avocadoes, red onion, dill and lemon juice. Season with salt and pepper. Mash everything together with a fork until chunky.

Let's assemble the tower!

Place a large cookie cutter on a plate. Layer the avocado mixture inside the cookie cutter followed by a layer of the chopped salmon on top. Carefully remove the cookie cutter to reveal the shaped tower. Top with the prawns and micro herbs.

CHICKEN NACHOS

SERVES 4

2 Tbsp oil
1 small onion, finely chopped
1 clove garlic, minced
1 Tbsp mild curry powder
2 chicken breasts, boiled in chicken stock and shredded
1 Tbsp chicken spice
1 × 410g can chopped tomatoes
1 packet tortilla chips
1 cup grated mozzarella cheese
Fresh parsley, finely chopped, to garnish

Preheat the oven to 160°C.

In a pan, heat the oil over medium heat. Add the onion and garlic, and sauté for 2 minutes, or until the onion is golden and caramelised. Stir in the curry powder and shredded chicken. Season with chicken spice, then add the canned tomatoes. Mix well. Cook for 3–5 minutes, or until the liquid has reduced, then set aside.

Spread a layer of tortilla chips at the base of an ovenproof dish. Top with the chicken and tomato mixture, then sprinkle over the grated cheese. Place in the oven for 3–5 minutes, or until the cheese has melted. Garnish with finely chopped fresh parsley.

VEGETABLE COCKTAIL SKEWERS

MAKES 8–10

8–10 cocktail skewers
1 large cucumber, thinly sliced into ribbons
2 cups cherry tomatoes
2 cups pitted olives
2–3 carrots, sliced

Thread the vegetables onto the skewers, alternating the vegetables.

Serve with Hummus (see p. 134).

DEVILLED EGGS

SERVES 4

4 eggs
2 Tbsp plain cream cheese
Handful chopped fresh parsley
Salt and pepper, to taste
Smoked paprika, to garnish

Boil the eggs for 12 minutes, then remove from the boiling water and transfer to a bowl filled with ice water. When the eggs have cooled, peel and discard the shells.

Cut the boiled eggs in half lengthways. Scoop out the yolks and add to a bowl. To the same bowl, add the cream cheese and chopped parsley, and season with salt and pepper. Mash everything together until well combined. Use a teaspoon to fill the empty boiled egg halves with the mixture. Alternatively, you can use a piping bag. Garnish with a sprinkling of smoked paprika and serve.

Vegetable Cocktail Skewers

Devilled Eggs

BAKERY

I must confess... baking is not my strongest point and I'll tell you why – it's too scientific for me. If you miss one step or don't get the oven temperature just right, believe me, your cake is gone! But, I love it. What I especially love about baking is the delicious smell in the home, one that always takes me back to my mom's kitchen.

SCONES

MAKES 50–60

8 cups cake wheat flour
1 cup white sugar
10 tsp baking powder
500g baking margarine, cut into cubes and softened to room temperature
2 cups amasi
4 large eggs, divided
2 tsp caramel essence

Preheat the oven to 190°C.

In a bowl, combine the flour, sugar and baking powder. Add the baking margarine and mix it into the dry ingredients using your fingertips, until the mixture resembles breadcrumbs. Set aside.

In another bowl, mix together the amasi, 3 eggs and the caramel essence until combined. Pour the wet-ingredient mixture into the dry-ingredient mixture. Mix with a wooden spoon until the dough just comes together.

Dust your work surface with flour and transfer the dough to your surface. Shape the dough into a ball, then use a rolling pin to roll it out to about 4cm thick. Dust the top with more flour, if necessary, to make sure the dough doesn't stick to the rolling pin. Use a cookie cutter to cut the dough into approximately 5cm circles, then transfer to a greased baking tray.

Lightly whisk the remaining egg. Brush the tops of the dough with the egg wash. Transfer to the oven and bake for 20 minutes, or until golden brown. Serve with jam and cream, or grated cheese.

HOT BAKED BLUEBERRY PUDDING

SERVES 6–8

2 eggs
¼ cup oil
1½ cups plain yoghurt
½ cup castor sugar
2 Tbsp vanilla essence
1½ cups self-raising flour
Pinch of salt
2 cups fresh blueberries, divided

Preheat the oven to 160°C. Grease a 30cm pie dish and set aside.

In a bowl, whisk together the eggs, oil, yoghurt, castor sugar and vanilla essence. Sift in the flour and salt, and mix well. Fold in 1 cup of the blueberries, then pour the mixture into the prepared pie dish. Top with the remaining berries. Bake for 45 minutes, or until golden brown. Serve warm.

MALVA PUDDING

SERVES 6

FOR THE PUDDING

30g butter
1 cup castor sugar
2 eggs
1 cup apricot jam
2 Tbsp vinegar
2 cups self-raising flour
Pinch of salt
1 cup milk

FOR THE SAUCE

3 Tbsp vanilla essence
100ml brandy
60g butter
1 cup milk

Preheat the oven to 180°C. Grease a 28 × 30cm rectangular, or 23 cm round, baking dish, with nonstick spray or oil.

Using an electric mixer, cream the butter, castor sugar and eggs together in a bowl. Mix in the jam and vinegar.

Sift the flour into a separate bowl and add the salt. Add the flour to the creamed butter and jam mixture. Mix using a wooden spoon, while slowly pouring in the milk. Pour the mixture into the prepared baking dish. Bake for 55 minutes, or until golden brown.

In the meantime, make the sauce. Add all the ingredients to a small saucepan over medium heat and bring to a boil, stirring frequently. Simmer until thickened. Pour the sauce over the malva pudding as it comes out of the oven and serve hot. Serve with custard.

CHOCOLATE FUDGE PUDDINGS

SERVES 4

100g butter,
plus extra for greasing
100g 70% dark chocolate
2 eggs
1 tsp vanilla essence
2 Tbsp cocoa powder
⅓ cup cake wheat flour
1 tsp baking powder
¼ cup castor sugar

Preheat the oven to 180°C. Grease 4 small ramekins with butter.

Fill a small, deep saucepan halfway with water and bring it to a simmer over low heat. Place a heatproof bowl in the saucepan. Make sure that there is space between the water and the bowl. (This is called a double boiler.) Add the chocolate and butter to the bowl, and allow it to melt gently, stirring frequently. Remove from the heat and allow to cool slightly (about 1 minute – the mixture mustn't be cool enough to harden, but it mustn't be so hot that the eggs cook when added).

To the melted chocolate and butter mixture, add the eggs and vanilla essence. Sift in the cocoa powder, flour, baking powder and castor sugar. Mix well. Pour the mixture equally among the prepared ramekins. Bake for 6–8 minutes, or until the tops have formed a crust.

Use a table knife to loosen the sides of the puddings from the ramekins and flip them over onto individual plates. Serve warm with ice cream.

HOT CROSS BUNS

MAKES 12

10g instant dry yeast
1 cup castor sugar
1 cup lukewarm milk
4 cups cake wheat flour
1 tsp salt
1 Tbsp ground cinnamon
1 cup raisins
2 eggs
100ml melted butter

FOR THE CROSS
½ cup self-raising flour
200ml milk

Preheat the oven to 180°C.

In a bowl, mix together the yeast, castor sugar and milk. Stir, then cover with cling wrap or a kitchen towel. Set aside for 5–10 minutes, or until it foams.

Sift the flour and salt into a bowl, then add the cinnamon and raisins. Add the eggs, then pour in the melted butter and yeast mixture. Mix, then knead for about 10 minutes, until a dough forms. Cover with cling wrap or a kitchen towel, and place in a warm spot for 1 hour, or until doubled in size.

Knock down the dough to remove the air pockets, then knead again for 2–3 minutes. Break the dough into tennis ball-sized balls and place on a greased baking tray.

To make the cross, mix the self-raising flour with the milk until well combined, then add the mixture to a piping bag. Pipe a cross onto the tops of the buns, then transfer to the oven to bake for 30–40 minutes, or until golden brown.

CARROT AND GINGER CAKE

MAKES 1 LARGE 24–26cm SINGLE-LAYER CAKE OR 1 SMALLER 22cm DOUBLE-LAYER CAKE

1 cup pecan nuts
2 cups cake flour
1 Tbsp baking powder
2 tsp bicarbonate of soda
Pinch of salt
2 tsp ground cinnamon
2 tsp ground ginger
2 tsp mixed spice
4 eggs
1½ cups soft brown sugar
1¼ cups oil
2 tsp vanilla essence
2 cups grated carrot

FOR THE ICING
200g cream cheese, room temperature
100g butter, softened
2 cups icing sugar, sifted
2 tsp lemon juice

Lightly spray or brush a 24–26cm round cake tin or 2 × 22cm round cake tins with a little oil. Line the base of the tin/s with baking paper.

Place the pecan nuts in a plastic sandwich bag or Ziploc bag and use a rolling pin to crush them into small chunks. If you like, reserve some of the nuts to decorate the top of the cake.

Preheat the oven to 170°C.

Sift the flour, baking powder, bicarbonate of soda, salt, cinnamon, ginger and mixed spice into a large mixing bowl.

In another bowl, beat the eggs, brown sugar, oil and vanilla essence. Fold the wet-ingredient mixture into the dry-ingredient mixture until just combined.

Fold the crushed pecan nuts and grated carrot into the cake batter, then pour the batter into the prepared cake tin/s. Bake on the centre rack of the oven for 45–50 minutes for a large cake, or 35–37 minutes for 2 smaller cakes.

Test for readiness by inserting a skewer into the centre of each cake; it should come out clean. When done, allow to cool in the tins for 5 minutes, then turn them out onto a wire rack to cool completely.

To make the icing, beat the cream cheese with the butter. Slowly add the icing sugar and lemon juice, and continue to beat until smooth and creamy. Spread all of the icing over the top of the cooled, large cake. Alternatively, if you've made a smaller, double-layer cake, sandwich the two cooled cakes together with some of the icing and use the rest to ice the top. Decorate with the reserved pecan nuts.

CONDENSED MILK AND PECAN NUT SHEET CAKE

MAKES 1
18 × 28cm CAKE

2 eggs
¼ cup oil
1½ cups plain yoghurt
1 cup condensed milk
2 Tbsp vanilla essence
1½ cups self-raising flour
Pinch of salt
1 cup chopped pecan nuts, divided

Preheat the oven to 160°C. Grease an 18 × 28cm baking tin.

In a bowl, mix the eggs, oil, yoghurt, condensed milk and vanilla essence. Sift in the flour and salt, and mix well. Fold half of the pecan nuts into the batter. Pour the batter into the prepared baking tin. Sprinkle over the remaining pecan nuts. Bake for 45 minutes, until golden brown, or until a skewer inserted into the centre comes out clean.

MARBLE BUNDT CAKE

**MAKES 1
25cm CAKE**

4 eggs
1 cup castor sugar
1 cup milk
1 cup sunflower oil
1 Tbsp vanilla essence
Pinch of salt
2 cups cake wheat flour
2 tsp baking powder
½ cup cocoa powder

Preheat the oven to 180°C. Grease a 25cm bundt cake tin.

In a bowl, whisk together the eggs, castor sugar, milk, oil, vanilla essence and salt until well combined. Sift in the flour and baking powder, and mix well.

Pour half the batter into a separate bowl. To this bowl, sift in the cocoa powder and mix.

Pour half the vanilla batter into the prepared cake tin, followed by half the chocolate batter. Pour in the remaining vanilla and chocolate batters, alternating between the two. Use a wooden skewer to gently swirl the two batters together. Transfer to the oven and bake for 35–40 minutes, or until a skewer inserted into the cake comes out clean.

RED VELVET CUPCAKES

MAKES 12 CUPCAKES

1¼ cups cake wheat flour
½ tsp baking powder
1 Tbsp cocoa powder
Pinch of salt
60g soft butter
¾ cup white sugar
½ cup oil
2 eggs
1 tsp vanilla essence
1–2 Tbsp red food colouring
½ cup buttermilk

FOR THE CREAM CHEESE ICING

125g (½ tub) plain cream cheese
1 packed cup icing sugar
1 tsp lemon juice
Fresh raspberries, to decorate

Preheat the oven to 180°C. Line a 12-cup muffin tray with cupcake liners.

Sift the flour, baking powder, cocoa powder and salt into a mixing bowl. Set aside.

In a separate bowl, use an electric mixer to beat the butter and sugar together until creamy. Add the oil, eggs, vanilla essence and red food colouring, and beat until combined. Add half the dry-ingredient mixture and half the buttermilk, and beat on a lower speed. Then, add the remaining dry-ingredient mixture and buttermilk, and beat until just combined.

Spoon the batter into the cupcake liners and bake for 15 minutes. They should be ready when the tops are springy, and a toothpick inserted into the centre comes out clean. Allow to cool for 5 minutes in the tray, then transfer the cupcakes to a wire rack to cool completely.

To make the cream cheese icing, beat the cream cheese, icing sugar and lemon juice together in a bowl until smooth. Spoon the mixture into a piping bag fitted with a star nozzle. Alternatively, use a plastic sandwich bag or Ziploc bag and snip the tip off one of the corners. Pipe the icing onto the top of each cupcake in a spiral, then finish off by decorating each one with a fresh raspberry.

SWEET TREATS & DRINKS

Honestly, I don't have much of a sweet tooth, but my husband and kids do. Whatever dessert recipe I develop, they are the ones who look forward to giving it their approval.

SWEET TREATS

KOEKSISTERS

MAKES 10–12

2 cups cake wheat flour
1 tsp baking powder
1 tsp salt
100g butter, room temperature
1 egg
½ cup milk
4 cups oil

FOR THE SYRUP

1 cup castor sugar
1 cup water
½ cup apricot jam
100ml lemon juice

In a bowl, mix together the flour, baking powder and salt. Add the butter, egg and milk, and mix well using your hands, until a smooth, elastic dough forms.

Dust your work surface with flour. Place the dough on the floured surface and use a rolling pin to roll it out in a rectangle about 5mm thick. Cut the dough lengthways into strips about 4cm wide and 8cm long. Keeping about 1cm at the top intact, cut the large strip of dough lengthways into 3 smaller, even strips. Then, plait the 3 strips of dough loosely, to give the dough room to expand when fried. Press the cut ends firmly together to seal and set aside.

Heat the oil in a large saucepan over high heat. Deep-fry the koeksisters for 4–5 minutes, or until golden brown. Remove from the oil and transfer to a plate lined with paper towel while you make the syrup.

To make the syrup, stir all the syrup ingredients together in a pan over medium heat. Simmer until thickened, then allow to cool before dipping in the koeksisters, making sure they are evenly coated.

OREO ICE CREAM

SERVES 6

2 cups fresh cream
½ cup condensed milk
8 Oreo cookies, crushed

In a bowl, using an electric hand mixer, whisk the cream until it is thick. Fold in the condensed milk and crushed Oreos. Cover with cling wrap, making sure that it touches the surface of the mixture. Transfer to a freezer-safe container, and freeze for 2 hours, or until set.

KIWI FRUIT SORBET

SERVES 1

6 kiwi fruit, peeled, cut into chunks, and frozen for at least 4–6 hours
1 Tbsp lemon juice
¼ cup golden syrup or honey
Ice water (optional)

Add the frozen kiwi fruit to the jug of a blender, along with the lemon juice and golden syrup or honey. Blend until smooth (you might need to add a few tablespoons of ice water to assist the blending). Transfer the mixture to a freezer-safe dish and freeze for 30 minutes, or until set.

MANGO AND BUBBLES SORBET

SERVES 1

2 cups diced fresh mango
¼ cup golden syrup
1 cup sparkling white wine

Add all the ingredients to the jug of a blender and blend until well combined and smooth. Pour the mixture into a freezer-safe dish. Cover with cling wrap and freeze for 2 hours, or until set.

RASPBERRY SORBET

SERVES 1

2 cups frozen raspberries
1 Tbsp lemon juice
½ cup white sugar
1 cup soda water

Add the frozen raspberries to the jug of a blender, along with the lemon juice, sugar and soda water. Blend until smooth. Transfer the mixture to a freezer-safe dish and freeze for 30 minutes, or until set.

DRINKS

*Did someone say 'drinks'?
A good drink is always great for sundowners,
or to reward yourself with something refreshing at the end of the week.*

WHISKEY SOUR

SERVES 1

2 Tbsp whiskey or bourbon
2 Tbsp lemon juice
2 Tbsp honey
½ cup of crushed ice
1 egg white
2 ice cubes, to serve
Lemon peel, to decorate

Add the whiskey, lemon juice, honey, crushed ice and egg white to a cocktail shaker, and shake until properly chilled. Strain into a glass over the ice cubes and decorate with the lemon peel.

MINT MOJITO

SERVES 1

Handful fresh mint leaves
¼ cup white rum
2 Tbsp lime cordial
¼ cup golden syrup
1 cup soda water
1 cup crushed ice
Sprig of mint, to decorate

Gently muddle the mint leaves in a highball glass. Add the white rum, lime cordial, golden syrup and soda water, and mix well. Add crushed ice, and stir briefly. Decorate with a sprig of mint.

LONG ISLAND ICED TEA

SERVES 1

1 Tbsp vodka
1 Tbsp white rum
1 Tbsp gin
1 Tbsp golden syrup
1 Tbsp lemon juice
1 cup cola, plus extra
1 cup crushed ice
1–2 slices fresh lemon, to decorate

Combine all ingredients in a tall glass. Briefly stir to combine. Top with an extra splash of cola. Decorate with a lemon slice.

PIÑA COLADA

SERVES 1

1 cup chopped fresh pineapple, plus an extra slice to decorate
100ml pineapple juice
2 Tbsp white rum
2 Tbsp castor sugar
2 Tbsp coconut milk
Handful of ice cubes

Add all the ingredients to the jug of a blender and blend until well combined and smooth. Garnish with a slice of pineapple.

SWEET TREATS & DRINKS

A DAY IN THE OFFICE

I left my IT job for pots and pans, yet I always found myself stuck working behind the computer! It became clear to me that I needed someone to help me manage the admin component of my new career path, and that's how I came to have a manager. I met Mabatho when I started my culinary journey. She used to attend my cooking classes, and our relationship grew from there. With Mabatho steering the ship, I could devote my attention to what I love and do best – cooking. When I *am* working on my computer, I'm either brainstorming ideas with Mabatho or developing recipes.

My day in the office looks very different to what it did when I worked in IT. Now I have my own brand, which requires me to be in the kitchen most of the time, rather than in an office. Usually, Mabatho is the first person I speak to in the morning, whether it's to remind me of what I need to post on social media, or to go through the meetings for the day on my calendar. She really makes my life easier and my workload lighter. Our journey together has been a fruitful and heart-warming one.

Life is better in pairs. I couldn't have accomplished all that I have without Mabatho's help. Sometimes things get too busy, but having her by my side makes everything feel doable. Thank you, Mabatho, for being part of my brand, and for not trying to change me but accepting me for who I am.

RECIPE INDEX

Asian seafood fried rice 86
Asian sesame dressing 131
atchaar, Mango 143
Avocado, prawn and salmon tower 163
Bacon and pepper pasta salad 149
bacon potato salad, Green bean and 108
bacon rice balls, Mozzarella and 154
Bacon-wrapped whole chicken 94
Baked goods (sweet & savoury)
   Carrot and ginger cake 180
   Chicken and bacon crustless mini quiches 14
   Chocolate fudge puddings 177
   Condensed milk and pecan nut sheet cake 183
   Hot baked blueberry pudding 172
   Hot cross buns 178
   Malva pudding 174
   Marble bundt cake 184
   Red velvet cupcakes 187
   Scones 171
   Soft bread rolls 146
Balsamic vinegar marinade 139
Bean and chickpea bulgur wheat salad 41

Bean, and bacon potato salad Green 108
Beans, Samp and 114
Béchamel sauce 32, 53
beef and vegetables, Roast 107
Beef curry 59
beef tripe, Herbed 119
Beetroot, feta and pine nut salad 101
bites with sweet chilli sauce, Super-easy chicken and bacon 160
Blanched veggies 31
Blue cheese sauce 127
blueberry pudding, Hot baked 172
bread rolls, Soft 146
bread, Steamed 117
Breakfast meals
   Chicken and bacon crustless mini quiches 14
   Chicken quesadilla 21
   Granola 12
   Peanut butter oats 17
   Pickled fish 24
   Tomato shakshuka 18
   Vegetarian omelette 23
Brown rice and halloumi salad 35
bulgur wheat salad, Bean and chickpea 41
bundt cake, Marble 184
bunny chow, Mutton 56
buns, Hot cross 178

burger, Pulled pork belly 65
butterflied chicken, Lemon and herb 72
butternut pasta, Lamb and 53
butternut, Orange-cinnamon roasted 97
cabbage, Uphuthu and 121
cake, Carrot and ginger 180
cake, Condensed milk and pecan nut sheet 183
cake, Marble bundt 184
Carrot and ginger cake 180
cheese dressing, Creamy blue 130
cheese sauce, Blue 127
Cheesy-mustard mashed potatoes 142
Chicken
   Bacon-wrapped whole chicken 94
   Chicken and bacon crustless mini quiches 14
   Chicken and mushroom pie 76
   Chicken and rice stir-fry 75
   Chicken breast coated with couscous 79
   Chicken nachos 164
   Chicken quesadilla 21
   Grilled chicken leg quarters 80
   Inkukhu yase khaya with a twist (Hardbody chicken) 113

Lemon and herb butterflied chicken 72
Spiced-up chicken wings 158
Super-easy chicken and bacon bites with sweet chilli sauce 160
Tandoori grilled chicken wings 159
Chicken and bacon crustless mini quiches 14
Chicken and mushroom pie 76
Chicken and rice stir-fry 75
Chicken breast coated with couscous 79
Chicken nachos 164
Chicken quesadilla 21
chicken, Hardbody 113
chickpea bulgur wheat salad, Bean and 41
Chimichurri 127
Chocolate fudge puddings 177
chops, Sweet and sour pork 66
coleslaw, Mustard-mayo 98
Condensed milk and pecan nut sheet cake 183
couscous, Chicken breast coated with 79
Cream cheese icing 180, 187
Creamy blue cheese dressing 130
Creamy peppercorn sauce 126
Creamy samp with mushrooms 143
Creamy spinach and mushrooms 102
cupcakes, Red velvet 187
curry, Beef 59
Deep-fried hake 89
Desserts see Sweet treats
Devilled eggs 166
Dips see Sauces, dressings, dips & marinades
Dressings see Sauces, dressings, dips & marinades

Drinks
   Long Island iced tea 197
   Mint mojito 196
   Piña colada 197
   Whiskey sour 196
eggs, Devilled 166
feta and pine nut salad, Beetroot, 101
Feta cheese dip 135
fillet, Stuffed pork 69
Fish see Seafood
fudge puddings, Chocolate 177
ginger cake, Carrot and 180
Glazed pork belly 71
Granola 12
Green bean and bacon potato salad 108
Green salad, The 42
Grilled chicken leg quarters 80
grilled chicken wings, Tandoori 159
Guacamole 135
Hake and prawns in a lemon and mustard butter sauce 85
Hake, Deep-fried 89
hake, Roasted baby 104
halloumi salad, Brown rice and 35
Hardbody chicken 113
herb butterflied chicken, Lemon and 72
herb marinade, Lemon and 139
herb salad, Tomato and 38
Herbed beef tripe 119
Hollandaise sauce 126
Honey-mustard dressing 36
Hot baked blueberry pudding 172
Hot cross buns 178
Hummus 134
ice cream, Oreo 193
Icing (cream cheese) 180, 187
Inkukhu yase khaya with a twist 113

Jalapeño dip 135
kebabs in a herby yoghurt sauce, Lamb 51
Kiwi fruit sorbet 194
Koeksisters 190
Lamb and butternut pasta 53
lamb chops, Thyme and mustard 54
Lamb kebabs in a herby yoghurt sauce 51
Lamb knuckle stew 48
lasagne, Vegetable 32
leg quarters, Grilled chicken 80
Lemon and herb butterflied chicken 72
Lemon and herb marinade 139
Lemon and mustard butter sauce 85
Lemon butter sauce 82
liver, Spicy ox 62
Long Island iced tea 197
Malva pudding 174
Mango and bubbles sorbet 194
Mango atchaar 143
Marble bundt cake 184
Marinades see Sauces, dressings, dips & marinades
mint marinade, Yoghurt and 138
Mint mojito 196
mojito, Mint 196
Mozzarella and bacon rice balls 154
mushroom pie, Chicken and 76
Mushroom risotto 44
Mushroom sauce 60
Mushrooms, Creamy samp with 143
mushrooms, Creamy spinach and 102
mustard dressing, Wholegrain 130

RECIPE INDEX | 203

mustard mashed potatoes, Cheesy- 142
Mustard sauce 127
Mustard-mayo coleslaw 98
Mutton bunny chow 56
nachos, Chicken 164
oats, Peanut butter 17
omelette, Vegetarian 23
Orange-cinnamon roasted butternut 97
Oreo ice cream 193
Pasta dishes
   Bacon and pepper pasta salad 149
   Lamb and butternut pasta 53
   Vegetable lasagne 32
Peanut butter oats 17
pecan nut sheet cake, Condensed milk and 183
pepper pasta salad, Bacon and 149
peppercorn sauce, Creamy 126
Pickled fish 24
pie, Chicken and mushroom 76
Piña colada 197
pine nut salad, Beetroot, feta and 101
Pork see Red meat
Potato bake 142
potato salad, Green bean and bacon 108
potatoes, Cheesy-mustard mashed 142
prawn and salmon tower, Avocado 163
prawns in a lemon and mustard butter sauce, Hake and 85
Prego marinade 138
pudding, Hot baked blueberry 172
pudding, Malva 174
puddings, Chocolate fudge 177
Pulled pork belly burger 65
quesadilla, Chicken 21

quiches, Chicken and bacon crustless mini 14
Raspberry sorbet 194
Red meat
   Bacon and pepper pasta salad 149
   Bacon-wrapped whole chicken 94
   Beef curry 59
   Chicken and bacon crustless mini quiches 14
   Glazed pork belly 71
   Green bean and bacon potato salad 108
   Herbed beef tripe 119
   Lamb and butternut pasta 53
   Lamb kebabs in a herby yoghurt sauce 51
   Lamb knuckle stew 48
   Mozzarella and bacon rice balls 154
   Mutton bunny chow 56
   Pulled pork belly burger 65
   Roast beef and vegetables 107
   Rump steak with mushroom sauce 60
   Savoury rice 102
   Spicy ox liver 62
   Stuffed pork fillet 69
   Super-easy chicken and bacon bites with sweet chilli sauce 160
   Sweet and sour pork chops 66
   Thyme and mustard lamb chops 54
   Uphuthu ne klabishi (Uphuthu and cabbage) 121
Red velvet cupcakes 187
rice and halloumi salad, Brown 35
rice balls, Mozzarella and bacon 154

rice stir-fry, Chicken and 75
rice, Asian seafood fried 86
rice, Savoury 102
risotto, Mushroom 44
Roast beef and
 vegetables 107
Roasted baby hake 104
Rump steak with mushroom
 sauce 60
Salads & sides
 Bacon and pepper pasta
  salad 149
 Bean and chickpea bulgur
  wheat salad 41
 Beetroot, feta and pine nut
  salad 101
 Blanched veggies 31
 Brown rice and halloumi
  salad 35
 Cheesy-mustard mashed
  potatoes 142
 Creamy samp with
  mushrooms 143
 Creamy spinach and
  mushrooms 102
 Green bean and bacon
  potato salad 108
 Green salad, *The* 42
 Mango atchaar 143
 Mozzarella and bacon rice
  balls 154
 Mushroom risotto 44
 Mustard-mayo
  coleslaw 98
 Orange-cinnamon roasted
  butternut 97
 Potato bake 142
 Savoury rice 102
 Steamed green veggies
  with honey-mustard
  dressing 36
 Tomato and herb salad 38
salmon tower, Avocado,
 prawn and 163

Salmon with lemon butter
 sauce and toasted almond
 flakes 82
Samp and beans 114
samp with mushrooms,
 Creamy 143
Sauces, dressings, dips
 & marinades
 Asian sesame dressing 131
 Balsamic vinegar
  marinade 139
 Béchamel sauce 32, 53
 Blue cheese sauce 127
 Chimichurri 127
 Creamy blue cheese
  dressing 130
 Creamy peppercorn
  sauce 126
 dressing for Bacon and
  pepper pasta salad 149
 dressing for Bean and
  chickpea bulgur wheat
  salad 41
 dressing for Beetroot, feta
  and pine nut salad 101
 dressing for Brown rice and
  halloumi salad 35
 dressing for Green bean and
  bacon potato salad 108
 dressing for Green salad,
  The 42
 dressing for Mustard-mayo
  coleslaw 98
 Feta cheese dip 135
 Guacamole 135
 Herby yoghurt sauce 51
 Hollandaise sauce 126
 Honey-mustard dressing 36
 Hummus 134
 Jalapeño dip 135
 Lemon and mustard butter
  sauce 85
 Lemon butter sauce 82
 Mango atchaar 143

 Mushroom sauce 60
 Mustard sauce 127
 Prego marinade 138
 syrup for Koeksisters 190
 sauce for Malva pudding 174
 sauce for Spiced-up
  chicken wings 158
 Sweet chilli sauce 160
 Tzatziki dip 134
 Wholegrain mustard
  dressing 130
 Yoghurt and mint
  marinade 138
Savoury rice 102
Scones 171
Seafood (including fresh
 & seawater fish)
 Asian seafood fried rice 86
 Avocado, prawn and salmon
  tower 163
 Deep-fried hake 89
 Hake and prawns in a lemon
  and mustard butter
  sauce 85
 Pickled fish 24
 Roasted baby hake 104
 Salmon with lemon butter
  sauce and toasted almond
  flakes 82
sesame dressing, Asian 131
shakshuka, Tomato 18
Side dishes see Salads
 & sides
skewers, Vegetable
 cocktail 166
Snack foods
 Avocado, prawn and salmon
  tower 163
 Chicken and bacon
  crustless mini quiches 14
 Chicken nachos 164
 Devilled eggs 166
 Mozzarella and bacon rice
  balls 154

Spiced-up chicken wings 158
Super-easy chicken and
   bacon bites with sweet
   chilli sauce 160
Tandoori grilled chicken
   wings 159
Vegetable cocktail
   skewers 166
Soft bread rolls 146
sorbet, Kiwi fruit 194
sorbet, Mango and
   bubbles 194
sorbet, Raspberry 194
Spiced-up chicken wings 158
Spicy ox liver 62
spinach and mushrooms,
   Creamy 102
steak with mushroom sauce,
   Rump 60
Steamed bread 117
Steamed green veggies with
   honey-mustard dressing 36
stew, Lamb knuckle 48
stir-fry, Chicken and rice 75
Stuffed pork fillet 69
Super-easy chicken and
   bacon bites with sweet chilli
   sauce 160
Sweet and sour pork chops 66
Sweet treats
   Carrot and ginger cake 180
   Chocolate fudge
      puddings 177
   Condensed milk and pecan
      nut sheet cake 183
   Hot baked blueberry
      pudding 172
   Hot cross buns 178
   Kiwi fruit sorbet 194
   Koeksisters 190
   Malva pudding 174
   Mango and bubbles
      sorbet 194
   Marble bundt cake 184

   Oreo ice cream 193
   Raspberry sorbet 194
   Red velvet cupcakes 187
   Scones 171
Tandoori grilled chicken
   wings 159
tea, Long Island iced 197
Thyme and mustard lamb
   chops 54
Tomato and herb salad 38
Tomato shakshuka 18
Traditional local dishes
   Hardbody chicken 113
   Herbed beef tripe 119
   Inkukhu yase khaya with
      a twist 113
   Mutton bunny chow 56
   Samp and beans 114
   Spicy ox liver 62
   Ujeqe (Steamed bread) 117
   Uphuthu ne klabishi
      (Uphuthu and cabbage)
      121
tripe, Herbed beef 119
Tzatziki dip 134
Ujeqe 117
Uphuthu and cabbage 121
Uphuthu ne klabishi 121
Vegetable cocktail skewers 166
Vegetable lasagne 32
Vegetarian
   Bean and chickpea bulgur
      wheat salad 41
   Beetroot, feta and pine
      nut salad 101
   Blanched veggies 31
   Brown rice and halloumi
      salad 35
   Cheesy-mustard mashed
      potatoes 142
   Creamy samp with
      mushrooms 143
   Creamy spinach and
      mushrooms 102

   Devilled eggs 166
   Green salad, *The* 42
   Mushroom risotto 44
   Mustard-mayo coleslaw 98
   Orange-cinnamon roasted
      butternut 97
   Potato bake 142
   Steamed green veggies
      with honey-mustard
      dressing 36
   Tomato and herb salad 38
   Tomato shakshuka 18
   Vegetable cocktail
      skewers 166
   Vegetable lasagne 32
   Vegetarian omelette 23
Vegetarian omelette 23
veggies with honey-mustard
   dressing, Steamed green 36
veggies, Blanched 31
Whiskey sour 196
Wholegrain mustard
   dressing 130
wings, Spiced-up chicken 158
wings, Tandoori grilled
   chicken 159
Yoghurt and mint marinade 138

Published in 2023 by Penguin Books,
an imprint of Penguin Random House South Africa (Pty) Ltd
Company Reg. No. 1953/000441/07

The Estuaries, 4 Oxbow Crescent, Century Avenue, Century City, 7441
PO Box 1144, Cape Town, 8000, South Africa

www.penguinrandomhouse.co.za

Copyright © in published edition:
Penguin Random House South Africa (Pty) Ltd 2023
Copyright © in text: Zanele van Zyl 2023
Copyright © in photographs:
Penguin Random House South Africa (Pty) Ltd 2023;
p1: © AstralAngel - stock.adobe.com

ISBN: 978-1-48590-151-8

Reprinted in 2025 (twice)

All rights reserved. No part of this publication may be reproduced, stored in a retrieval system or transmitted, in any form or by any means, electronic, mechanical, photocopying, recording or otherwise, without the prior written permission of the publishers and the copyright holders.

PUBLISHER: Beverley Dodd
MANAGING EDITOR: Aimee Sinclair
DESIGNER: Randall Watson
PROOFREADER: Cecilia Barfield
PHOTOGRAPHER: Henk Hattingh
STYLIST: Emma Wilson
ASSISTANTS: Kate Ferreira, Nicola Naude and Lulu Zokufa

Reproduction: Studio Repro

Printed and bound by Novus Print, South Africa

Making illegal copies of this publication, distributing them unlawfully or sharing them on social media without the written permission of the publisher may lead to civil claims or criminal complaints.

Protect the communities who are sustained by creativity.